DRAINING THE SWAMP

Can the US Survive the Last 100 Years
of Sociocommunist Societal Rot?

*A retrospective on the last 100 years of US sociopolitical evolution
…and what needs to be done about it*

*"The only thing necessary for the triumph of
evil is for good men to do nothing."*
Edmund Burke (1729–1797)

*"Life can only be understood backwards,
but it must be lived forwards."*
Soren Aabye Kierkegaard (1813–1855)

DAVID L. R. STEIN

PAGE PUBLISHING, INC.
New York, NY

First originally published by Page Publishing, Inc. 2017

ISBN 978-1-64082-583-3 (Paperback)
ISBN 978-1-64082-584-0 (Digital)

Printed in the United States of America

CONTENTS

PREFACE

The brainwashing of innocent and unsuspecting children ranks as one of the most evil and heinous crimes against humanity yet conceived by criminal minds. As the primary tool exploited by sociocommunists to subvert six thousand years of moral learning and teaching, it poses the greatest threat to civilized society ever faced by humankind. In the last century alone, it has been directly responsible for the slaughter of <u>more than eighty-five million people</u>[1]—approximately fifty million in WWII and twenty million in WWI, plus eight million in the Chinese Civil War, at least five million in the Russian Civil War, and more than one million in each of the Korean and the Vietnam wars—a total estimated to be greater than <u>the entire population of Europe (excluding Russia) at the dawn of the eighteenth century</u>[2].

In my own lifetime, I have witnessed its pernicious effects on US citizens, including my own children, whom I am embarrassed to admit could not be shielded from it. A few of the most brilliant among us—such as <u>David J. Horowitz</u>[3] and <u>Norman Podhoretz</u>[4]—are able to surmount their childhood brainwashing as a natural part of the human maturation process. Sadly, the vast majority of the populace lacks either the requisite eye-opening experiences or the intellectual capacity needed to throw off such brainwashing, with the inevitable result that they become its unwitting victims.

When I first undertook the task of writing the present account, it was intended solely for the benefit of my own children—as a kind of apology for my own failure to shield them from pernicious sociocommunist brainwashing conducted in the guise of education. It was only after discussing the project with some of my most-esteemed colleagues and friends that I endeavored to raise the alarm more broadly in the hope that, in some small way, I might help others better understand the existential threat the international sociocommunist conspiracy poses to continuation of the US as a constitutional democratic republic, in particular, and to civilized society, in general.

It's not enough to recognize the threat. What is needed is an understanding of the insidious and seductive appeal that sociocommunism has for the most vulnerable among us—namely: our defenseless, innocent, and unsuspecting children.

To paraphrase a once-famous comedienne, if any of what follows upsets you, please tell your friends.

INTRODUCTION

What Is Meant by "Sociocommunism"?

As used here, "sociocommunism" includes all variations of Marxist-inspired totalitarian political ideologies, including socialism, communism, and "progressivism." Indeed, distinguishing between socialism and communism is to make a distinction without a difference. As stressed by none other than <u>Vladimir Lenin</u>[5], socialism is but an immature form of communism.[1] As a political and economic theory of social organization, sociocommunism is built on the false promise of a utopian classless society. None other than <u>Karl Marx</u>[6] promised, "*From each according to his ability, to each according to his needs.*" Instead, history has shown that in practice sociocommunism's main purpose is to establish totalitarian government by a new ruling class of self-appointed, self-aggrandizing, self-perpetuating, self-righteous, self-serving, and unaccountable political elites.

Sociocommunism sacrifices individual freedoms for the sake of myriad presumed larger social benefits and governmental prerogatives. The first thing sacrificed is intellectual freedom. There is ample evidence of that fact today on US college and university campuses where kangaroo courts and sociocommunist thought-police preclude free speech by promulgating the false dogma of "political correctness" as the only acceptable form of human discourse.

---

[1]   "*The goal of socialism is communism.*" Vladimir Ilyich Ulyanov, aka Lenin

"Dedicating the memorial at <u>Gettysburg</u>[7], <u>Abraham Lincoln</u>[8] said of America, 'We are now engaged in a great Civil War, testing whether this nation or any nation so conceived and so dedicated can long endure.' Those words are true again. I believe that we are again engaged in a great civil war, a cultural war that's about to hijack your birthright to think and say what resides in your heart. I fear you no longer trust the pulsing lifeblood of liberty inside you ... the stuff that made this country rise from wilderness into the miracle that it is. ... In his book, 'THE END OF SANITY,' Martin Gross writes that 'blatantly irrational behavior is rapidly being established as the norm in almost every area of human endeavor. There seem to be new customs, new rules, new antiintellectual theories regularly foisted on us from every direction. Underneath, the nation is roiling. Americans know something without a name is undermining the nation, turning the mind mushy when it comes to separating truth from falsehood and right from wrong. And they don't like it.' ... Before you claim to be a champion of free thought, tell me: Why did political correctness originate on America's campuses? And why do you continue to tolerate it? Why do you, who're supposed to debate ideas, surrender to their suppression?" <u>Charlton Heston</u>[9], <u>*Winning the Cultural War*,</u> [10] Address to the Harvard Law School Forum, February 16, 1999

That *"something without a name"* in the excerpt above is socio-communism. Together with its other characteristically fiendish methods, sociocommunism's laser-like focus on the brainwashing of children[2]—i.e., anyone under the age of <u>twenty-five</u>[11] when the

---

[2]   *"Give me four years to teach the children and the seed I have sown will never be uprooted."* Vladimir Ilyich Ulyanov, aka Lenin

human brain is not yet fully developed[3] and has not yet acquired sufficient worldly experience to critically examine other's worldviews—undoubtedly makes it the most evil, lethal, and pernicious political and economic theory yet devised. Its track record of successfully overthrowing existing governments by insidiously brainwashing children and exploiting mass media to stealthily and systematically corrupt and take over educational and governmental institutions is a twentieth-century phenomenon without historical precedent. Sadly, the debilitating sociocommunist disease has been permitted to spread freely throughout the US for more than one hundred years.

Is the US Now on the Brink of a Social Revolution?

The US is now divided roughly equally between two principal political factions that are constantly at each other's throats ideologically, namely:[4]

- Atheistic globalist sociocommunists (a.k.a. leftists, liberals, progressives, and secular progressives) and their sympathizers who favor changing or reinterpreting the US Constitution to conform to their ideology, as well as massive federal and world government and increased spending on socialist programs, and

---

[3] In a bizarre twist of fate, the human species achieves sexual maturity in half the time needed to achieve mental maturity. Evidently, the power to procreate was more important to human survival in the past than an ability to think. As that is highly unlikely to be the case in technologically-advanced future societies, its unfortunate evolutionary legacy could now well pose a huge threat to the future survival of the species. That will be especially true if the US continues to allow sociocommunists to brainwash its children instead of educating them.

[4] Note that leftists, liberals, progressives, or secular progressives (aka sociocommunists) and conservatives are the contemporary terms for what Ludwig Von Mises termed Communists and anti-Communists[17] nearly one hundred years ago.

- God-fearing conservatives who want to return the country to federalism, strict adherence to the US Constitution, and a robust free-market economy unencumbered by bloated and costly federal government bureaucracies.

With roughly two-thirds of its citizens now believing the US is moving in the wrong political direction, it's clear Donald Trump was elected to the presidency as a change candidate. However, based on the 2016 popular vote, it's fair to say the US is split down the middle as to exactly how its direction should be changed. Thus, the US is more politically polarized today than it has been at any time since the Civil War.

While there are large segments of both the Democrat and Republican parties who insist all is well and there is no need for substantive changes, that view was soundly repudiated by the 2016 presidential election of Donald Trump. That reality poses an obvious question: How is it that large segments of both the Democrat and Republican parties can be in agreement that drastic changes are not needed when a plurality of the electorate believes otherwise? The answer is that large segments of both political parties are members of what Angelo Codevilla[12] terms the "ruling[13]" class and Peggy Noonan[14] terms the "protected[15]" class, and that class has benefited mightily from past globalist sociocommunist government policies and would benefit from a continuation of such policies. Ms. Noonan summarizes the difference between the "protected" class and what she terms the "unprotected" class succinctly as, "*The protected make public policy. The unprotected live in it.*" In other words, the protected class sold out the unprotected class for their own personal gain. Put another way, the ruling class comprises government bureaucrats plus all those colluding with them to secure a free ride for themselves at the expense of the unprotected class.

Of course, those who've gotten a free ride at others' expense for decades are not inclined to give it up voluntarily; hence, the disparity in worldviews. And because the ruling class has been making the government policies, which have been showering riches on themselves, it should surprise no one that the unprotected class—which includes the middle class and lower-income classes—has had quite enough of the unfairness and is beginning to demand changes. Indeed, the situation has reached a point where some believe the US is on the brink of a social revolution. Consider the following expert opinion.

> *"Because Republicans largely agree with Democrats that they need not take seriously the founders' Constitution, today's American regime is now what Max Weber had called the Tsarist regime on the eve of the Revolution: 'fake constitutionalism.' Because such fakery is self-discrediting and removes anyone's obligation to restrain his passions, it is a harbinger of revolution and of imperial power. ... We have stepped over the threshold of a revolution. It is difficult to imagine how we might step back, and futile to speculate where it will end. Our ruling class's malfeasance, combined with insult, brought it about. Donald Trump did not cause it and is by no means its ultimate manifestation. Regardless of who wins in 2016, this revolution's sentiments will grow in volume and intensity, and are sure to empower politicians likely to make Americans nostalgic for Donald Trump's moderation." After the Republic*[16] by Angelo Codevilla, the Claremont Review of Books, September 27, 2016

Note that Codevilla wrote that opinion more than a month before the 2016 presidential election, when conventional wisdom had it that Hillary Clinton would be elected instead of Donald Trump. Consequently, when he wrote that, Codevilla could not have known Trump would draw support from conservatives in both the Democrat and Republican parties over the strenuous objections of their sociocommunist factions—who most thought would prevail over Trump. Thus, Codevilla can be forgiven for not having limited his indictment to the progressive (a.k.a. globalist sociocommunist) factions of the Democrat and Republican parties.

To determine whether or not it's possible for the US to peacefully change from its present course, among other things, it's necessary to gauge the level of the electorate's dissatisfaction with the present course and whether or not that dissatisfaction is sufficient to motivate an effective sustained rebellion against the continuation of globalist sociocommunist policies.

How Great Is Dissatisfaction with the Status Quo in the US Today?

One example will suffice to illustrate the economic-unfairness grievances of the US unprotected class, namely: the $14 trillion (2016 US$) US trade deficit accumulated over the last forty years (see chart).

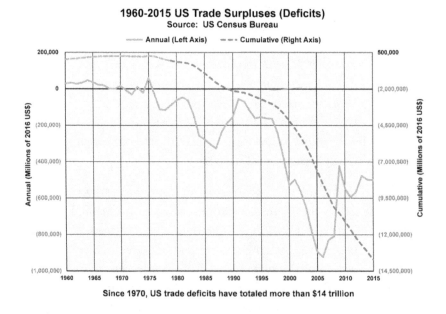

1960-2015 US Trade Surpluses (Deficits)
Source: US Census Bureau

Since 1970, US trade deficits have totaled more than $14 trillion

Globalist sociocommunists have benefited mightily from those huge trade deficits, but the same deficits have devastated US manufacturing industries. Areas surrounding Detroit, Michigan, bear silent witness to the devastation. In the 1950s, the Detroit area was one of the most affluent in the US with new factories springing up. Today, some of those same factories are more reminiscent of buildings in the Chernobyl Exclusion Zone[18]. What were shiny new factories forty or more years ago have since been reduced to rubble.

Money is the lifeblood of every economy; and just as a persistent chronic bloodletting will weaken any animal, a persistent chronic negative trade balance—while not equitably, ethically, or legally imposed—surely will be an egregious tax on the economy of any country foolish enough to suffer it for any protracted period of time. The $10.4 trillion (2016 US$) US trade deficit accumulated in just the thirty-three-year period of 1976 through 2008, plus approximately $1.3 trillion (2016 US$) of interest paid on that debt by the US Treasury over the same period, comprised essentially all of the $11.7 trillion (2016 US$) US national debt at the end of 2008—i.e., immediately prior to the Barack Obama[19] administration. That debt continues to place an enormous financial drain on the US economy. Imagine, if you can, how different the US economy would be in general, and US manufacturing industries would be in particular, if the US had insisted on demonstrably-fair trade over the last forty years.

Not only have the so-called "free trade" policies of globalist sociocommunists devastated US manufacturing industries, they have beggared the unprotected class as well. Free-trade fear-mongers suffer from the same kind of delusion as global-warming fear-mongers. Objective observers should realize that the pursuit of free trade between sovereign states is as problematic[5] as the pursuit of nuclear disarmament between sovereign states. The incentive to cheat is irresistible and politically overwhelming. As Trump rightly points out, what is needed is negotiated fair trade—i.e., "managed trade" which accounts for real-world realities, not the least of which is the need to preserve US manufacturing industries vital to sustaining middle-class jobs as well as the country's national defense and economic well-being.

---

[5] *"Based on the empirical evidence and world trade patterns, the validity of trade theories[22] is [highly] questionable and debatable as shown by the paradoxical findings. ... Trade theories fail to consider the demand side, marketing activities, and trade barriers. All of these can significantly alter trade patterns."*

Perhaps the US could afford to subsidize trade with the rest of the world for a couple of decades after World War II, but the US can't afford an ongoing Marshall Plan[20] for the entire world—whether or not the recipients believe they deserve it. Other developed countries (e.g., European Union countries) with more enlightened trade policies compete by levying tariffs on goods produced in countries with lower costs achieved through currency manipulations, government subsidies, lower living standards, etc. The self-serving and specious argument that much of the world prospered over the last forty years in spite of extensive fair-trade abuses should be recognized as a simple-minded sophism, which confuses correlations with causes and effects. It's akin to saying that the thievery which takes place in the stock market as a result of illegal and unethical trading practices is what makes stock prices increase over the long term.

Sadly, an even greater fleecing of the unprotected class in the US has been so successfully camouflaged from public view, the vast majority of US citizens are almost entirely unaware of it. Moreover, it's a direct consequence of the systematic devaluation of the US currency and the ever-increasing accumulation of US national debt made possible by the treacherous 1913 take-over of the US banking system by a cartel comprising a newly-created faux Federal Reserve Bank—owned and operated not by the US government but by the most powerful big-city banks—with the complicity of the Woodrow Wilson[21]administration. That historic perfidy stands as an unrivaled monument to the political malfeasance of a self-appointed, self-aggrandizing, self-perpetuating, self-righteous, self-serving, and unaccountable ruling class, yet it goes unpunished.

> "*In my lectures throughout this nation and in my appearances on many radio and television programs, I have sounded the toxin [tocsin] that the Federal Reserve System is not Federal; it has no reserves; and it is not a system at all, but rather, a criminal syndicate. From November 1910, when the conspirators met on Jekyll Island, Georgia, to the present time, the machinations of the Federal Reserve bankers have been shrouded in secrecy. Today [1991], that secrecy*

has cost the American people a three-trillion-dollar debt, with annual interest payments to these bankers amounting to some three-hundred-billion dollars per year, sums which stagger the imagination and, which in themselves, are ultimately unpayable. Officials of the Federal Reserve System routinely issue remonstrances to the public, much as the Hindu fakir pipes an insistent tune to the dazed cobra which sways its head before him, not to resolve the situation, but to prevent it from striking him. Such was the soothing letter written by Donald J. Winn, Assistant to the Board of Governors in response to an inquiry by a Congressman, the Honorable Norman D. Shumway, on March 10, 1983. Mr. Winn states that 'The Federal Reserve System was established by an act of Congress in 1913 and is not a private corporation.' On the next page, Mr. Winn continues, 'The stock of the Federal Reserve Banks is held entirely by commercial banks that are members of the Federal Reserve System.' He offers no explanation as to why the government has never owned a single share of stock in any Federal Reserve Bank or why the Federal Reserve System is not a private corporation when all of its stock is owned by private corporations.

American history in the twentieth century has recorded the amazing achievements of the Federal Reserve bankers. First, the outbreak of World War I, which was made possible by the funds available from the new central bank of the United States. Second, the Agricultural Depression of 1920. Third, the Black Friday Crash on Wall Street of October 1929 and the ensuing Great Depression. Fourth, World War II. Fifth, the conversion of the assets of the United States and its citizens from real property to paper assets from 1945 to the present, transforming a victorious America and foremost world power in 1945 to the world's largest debtor nation in 1990. Today [1991], this nation lies in economic ruins, devastated and destitute, in much the same dire straits in which Germany and Japan found themselves in 1945. Will Americans act to rebuild our nation, as Germany and Japan have done when they faced the identical conditions which we now face – or will we continue to be enslaved by the Babylonian debt-money system which was set up by the Federal Reserve Act in 1913 to complete our total destruction? This is the only question which we have to answer, and we do not have much time left to answer it."[6]

As shown in the chart on page 18 illustrating the annual deflation (inflation) rate in the value of the US dollar over the last one hundred years, one of the first actions taken by the owners of the newly created Federal Reserve Bank was to effect an egregious and nefarious deflation of the US currency—while securing their own reserves in gold bullion—that reduced the value of the US dollar by more than fifty percent in just seven years for the singular purpose of bankrupting the rural US banks, which at the time held a majority of the US currency due to the fact that the US economy was still dominated by the agricultural industry.

That treacherous and vicious criminal 1914–1920 assault on US rural banks by the owners of the Federal Reserve Bank accomplished its purpose by consolidating the country's wealth and gold stocks in their own banks, but it also plunged the entire US into the Agricultural Depression of 1920. The owners of the Federal Reserve Bank were then forced to rapidly reflate the US currency to pull the country out of the economic depression they had created. As the

---

6   From the 1991 Forward to *SECRETS OF THE FEDERAL RESERVE*[24] *(The London Connection)* by Eustace Mullins, first published in 1952 by Kasper and Horton, New York: "*The original book was the first nationally-circulated revelation of the secret meetings of the international bankers at Jekyll Island, Georgia, 1907-1910, at which place the draft of the Federal Reserve Act of 1913 was written.*"

big-city banks, having avoided bankruptcy, were suddenly flush with money, the rapid reflation of the US currency precipitated the decade of the Roaring Twenties. That euphoric decade ended with the infamous October 1929 stock-market crash, which plunged the US into the Great Depression,[7] thereby completing a deflation-reflation cycle[8] that immediately forced another just like it in the 1930s. In addition to creation of the Agricultural Depression of 1920 and the Roaring Twenties, the major deflation anomalies in the value of the US dollar—which are clearly visible in the chart—were created by the Great Depression, World War II, the Korean War, the Vietnam War, the 1973 OPEC oil embargo, the Jimmy Carter[23] administration, and the first Gulf War.

---

[7]   When Milton Friedman[25] and Anna Schwartz[26] wrote *A MONETARY HISTORY OF THE UNITED STATES, 1867-1960*[27] (or simply *Monetary History*) calling attention to these facts, "*the Federal Reserve Board responded internally with a lengthy critical review[28]. Such was their agitation that the Fed governors discontinued their policy of releasing minutes from the Board's meetings to the public. Additionally, they commissioned a counterhistory to be written (by Elmus R. Wicker) in the hope of detracting from Monetary History.*"

[8]   "*If the American people ever allow private banks to control the issue of their currency, first by inflation, then by deflation, the banks and corporations that will grow up around them will deprive the people of all property until their children wake up homeless on the continent their Fathers conquered ... I believe that banking institutions are more dangerous to our liberties than standing armies ... The issuing power should be taken from the banks and restored to the people, to whom it properly belongs.*" – Thomas Jefferson[29]

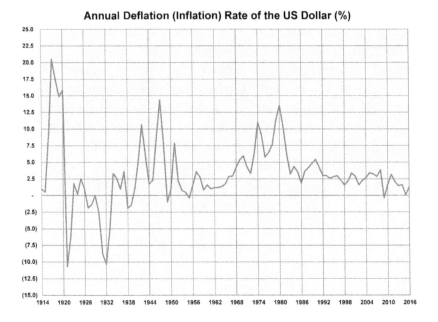

Annual Deflation (Inflation) Rate of the US Dollar (%)

As egregious as the Federal Reserve Bank's institutionalized and persistent devaluation of the US currency is, it's no more egregious than its printing of money to finance an ever-increasing US national debt—which is now more than $19.8 trillion[30] (2016 US$) and steadily rising. The printing of money has two evil consequences: the resulting price inflation further devalues the US currency, and it transfers wealth from the unprotected class to the protected class in the form of US Treasury interest payments on the government's mounting debt. Consequently, the devaluation of US currency by the Federal Reserve Bank not only places an enormous drain on the US treasury but, in the process, it places an egregious permanent parasitic stealth tax on every US citizen[9] who still owns some of that currency.

---

9   "*Financing government spending by increasing the quantity of money looks like magic, like getting something for nothing. ... the extra money printed is equivalent to a tax on money balances. The newly printed Federal Reserve notes are in effect receipts for taxes paid.*" – *MONEY MISCHIEF*[34] (Episodes in Monetary History) by Milton Friedman, Harcourt Brace & Company, 1994

The historical devaluation of the US dollar over the last one hundred years is illustrated in the chart below. Note the effects of the three reflation cycles corresponding to the Agricultural Depression, the Great Depression, and World War II. As shown in the chart, what was worth twenty-five US$ in 1913 is worth just one US$ today. Put another way, the US dollar has been devalued to one-twenty-fifth of its 1913 value. That is why a loaf of bread that cost 0.056 1913 US$ per pound in 1913 now costs 1.422 2016 US$ per pound[31]. For the same reason, much of the vaunted gains in US wages since 1913 are illusory. Consider that the average manufacturing wage was 0.22 1913 US$ per hour[32] in 1913, and is now 20.60 2016 US$ per hour[33]. More than one-fourth of that increase is due to devaluation of the US dollar. Arguably, an even better measure of the false sense of economic prosperity that results from devaluation of the US currency is the fact that a 1913 Saint-Gaudens Double Eagle gold coin with a face value of 20 US$ is now worth more than 1,100 2016 US$[35].

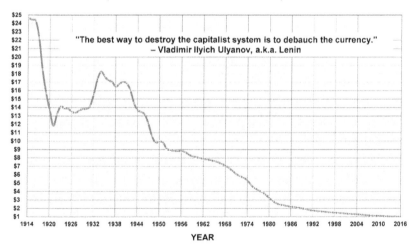

**Historical Devaluation of US Currency
(since creation of the FRB in 1913)**

"The best way to destroy the capitalist system is to debauch the currency."
– Vladimir Ilyich Ulyanov, a.k.a. Lenin

YEAR

Are the economic-unfairness grievances of the unprotected class sufficient to motivate a sustained rebellion against the protected class and continuation of its globalist sociocommunist tyrannies? By themselves, probably not. But when the many other grievances of the unprotected class—such as congressional, judicial, and presidential failures to defend the US Constitution; decaying public infrastructures; escalating criminal drug cultures in home communities; failed educational institutions; government failures to enforce laws and the rule of law; government-sanctioned attacks on personal choices and religions; rapidly escalating medical costs; skyrocketing college tuition costs; stagnant family incomes; sustained high-unemployment levels; et al—are taken into account, the answer is not obvious.

The Prospects for Substantive Changes in the Political Direction of the US

Was Codevilla serious about the US being on the brink of a social revolution, or was he simply issuing a tongue-in-cheek wake-up call? If he was serious, is his assessment correct? Is the US now on the brink of a social revolution? If so, is it a conservative counterrevolution intent on reversing the accelerating decline in personal liberties precipitated by one hundred years of rule by globalist sociocommunists? Can a Trump-inspired "velvet" conservative counterrevolution succeed? In the absence of such a "velvet" conservative counterrevolution, are there any other alternatives short of a "hot" revolution which would restore the US as a democratic republic? And what will determine the outcome? Before such questions can be addressed, an assessment is needed of the prospects for substantive changes in the political direction of the US.

While it's clear there will be substantive changes in administrative policies between the Barack Obama and Donald Trump administrations, it's far less clear whether or not there will be any substantive changes made in US educational and governmental institutions. Those bureaucracies have withstood attempted reforms in the past only to emerge largely unscathed, and—for really substantive changes to occur in the country's direction—they would need to change as well. Substantive changes in administrative policies by themselves will not be enough to arrest the country's momentum on its present course, to say nothing of charting a new course.

It's inconceivable that globalist sociocommunists will support a Trump-inspired "velvet" conservative counterrevolution. Instead, it's certain they will simply return to classical sociocommunist guerrilla-warfare tactics, while impatiently waiting for an opportunity to regain control of the US governmental agenda. There is something truly frightening about the demonstrated ability of large bureaucracies and political parties to withstand criticisms or changes initiated from the outside, and—to determine whether or not it's even possible for the US to change from its present course—it's necessary to first understand what brought its political parties and educational and governmental institutions to their present lamentable states.

HOW THE US ARRIVED
AT THIS JUNCTURE

A Historical Perspective

From Plato to the present, some intellectuals have been seduced into believing that they alone are fit to govern. Even if that were true, it begs the questions of how and through what mechanisms. These questions have led to experimentation with a variety of totalitarian models of government, predominantly communism and fascism (i.e., national socialism). While some contend there are important differences between the two, their similarities are vastly more important than their differences. Chief among their similarities is the presumed right of a few to govern the many—i.e., a firm commitment to statism. Consequently, both stand in stark contrast to the democratic-republic model of government in which the many are presumed able to govern themselves through democratically-elected representatives. Moreover—as demonstrated by the evolution of communism in Argentina, Cambodia, China, Cuba, Russia, Venezuela, Zimbabwe, et al—communism is easily transformed into fascism.

As an early twentieth-century European statesman actively engaged in attempting to help Europe find a better way forward after World War I, Albert Einstein[36] sought to find a way to circumvent the narrow nationalistic interests that were frustrating creations of a more-democratic Europe. His pursuit of a socialistic ideal failed, but

his efforts made him keenly aware of the inherent tendency of socialism to concentrate totalitarian power in the state.[10]

A primary purpose of sociocommunism is to achieve absolute
state control of educational and governmental institutions in order to
establish a new morality through systematic elimination of all historical, parental, and religious influence. In so doing, sociocommunism
abandons six thousand years of moral learning and teaching in favor
of avant-garde social engineering under the banner of progressivism.
Again, the implications[37] were not lost on Einstein.

> *"Of course, understanding of our fellow-beings is
> important. But this understanding becomes fruitful
> only when it is sustained by sympathetic feeling in
> joy and sorrow. The cultivation of this most import-
> ant spring of moral action is that which is left of
> religion when it has been purified of the elements of
> superstition. In this sense, religion forms an import-
> ant part of education, where it receives far too lit-
> tle consideration, and that little not sufficiently
> systematic.*
>
> *The frightful dilemma of the political world
> situation has much to do with this sin of omission on
> the part of our civilization. Without 'ethical culture'
> there is no salvation for humanity."* Albert Einstein

Survival instincts alone should be sufficient to warn that such
social engineering, however motivated and rationalized, is based on
the same kind of misguided pseudoscience as the nineteenth-century
racist eugenics[38] nonsense espoused by such luminaries as George
Bernard Shaw[39] and Woodrow Wilson, which pseudoscience led to
numerous twentieth-century communist and fascist genocidal atroc-

---

10 *"As to socialism[40], unless it is international to the extent of producing world government which controls all military power, it might more easily lead to wars than
capitalism, because it represents a still greater concentration of power."* – Albert
Einstein

ities that murdered tens of millions of innocents accused of being impediments to "progress."

With its promises of a utopian classless society, redistribution of wealth from the rich to the poor, and retribution for alleged grievances—all of which are nurtured and inculcated in the masses through carefully-crafted propaganda[11]—socialism is the most expedient means of inciting the masses to social revolution. However, once a socialist-inspired revolution has succeeded, communism is the most expedient means of impressing the masses into economic slavery by separating them from their property. Thus, Lenin's claim that "*The goal of socialism is communism*" is only a half-truth. As demonstrated by the fact there were no material differences between the modes of operation of the governments of the former Soviet Union (officially the Union of Soviet Socialist Republics) and the Third Reich, de facto fascism is the ultimate goal of communism, and—consequently—it's also the ultimate goal of socialism. The notion that communism and fascism are somehow polar opposites—as in extreme "left" and extreme "right"—is utter nonsense. And as both tend to deprive everyone but the ruling class of their property, sociocommunism is the fastest ROAD TO SERFDOM[42], as was clearly understood by Friedrich Hayek[43].

Tragically, the vast majority of the pathetic souls who work feverishly to bring about sociocommunist revolutions don't realize what is happening to them until it's too late. The US is now sliding dangerously close to a point of no return. If Codevilla is correct, then the choice is simply between two different kinds of revolutions, either a globalist sociocommunist take-over or a conservative coun-

---

[11] "*In watching the course of political events, I was always struck by the active part which propaganda played in them. I saw that it was an instrument, which the Marxist Socialists knew how to handle in a masterly way and how to put it to practical uses.*" – Adolf Hitler, *MEIN KAMPF*[41]

The modern term is "agitprop," which was coined in the former Soviet Union as a more descriptive term for political propaganda disseminated through mass media. A contraction for "agitation and propaganda," it evidently was not part of Hitler's vocabulary when he wrote *MEIN KAMPF*. However, it's clear from his disquisitions about propaganda that his meaning was the same.

terrevolution, which brings with it the reforms needed to reverse a sociocommunist slide into slavery.

Where It All Began

Angelo Codevilla's brilliant assessment[12] lays bare all that is wrong with the US and its self-appointed, self-aggrandizing, self-perpetuating, self-righteous, self-serving, and unaccountable ruling class; and he rightly points out that the majority of the sociocommunist societal rot in the US was not yet evident fifty years ago. However, it would be a serious mistake to believe that the advanced degree of societal rot now evident in US educational and governmental institutions was realized in just fifty years.

In fact, globalist sociocommunist conspiracies began more than one hundred years ago with the Progressive movements in Europe and the US. As progressivism was based on eugenics—or racism in its purest form—with its implicit ruling class, it's not surprising that the progressive movement in the US was eagerly embraced by *"the party of slavery, black codes, Jim Crow, and that miserable terrorist excrescence, the Ku Klux Klan."*[13] And given its historic roots as an elitist "white man's party[44]," it readily explains the Democrat party's love affair with statism. The fact that its thinly-veiled globalist sociocommunist ideology has not yet succeeded in overthrowing the US government is a tribute only to the achievement of the US Constitution and its framers. The US example is proof that sociocommunist conspiracies can go undeterred and undetected across many generations, thereby requiring extraordinary vigilance by its intended victims. The fact that more than one hundred years can be required for a sociocommunist conspiracy to succeed is what makes sociocommunism so extraordinarily dangerous and insidious.

---

12   *After the Republic*[48] by Angelo Codevilla, the *Claremont Review of Books*, September 27, 2016

13   *Whitewashing the Democratic* [sic] *Party's History*[49] by Mona Charen, *National Review*, June 26, 2015

In his book *CRISIS AND LEVIATHAN*[45], Robert Higgs[46] defines political "ideology" as follows: "*The 'softer' forms of knowledge— knowledge being understood here as simply what some people believe, whether others agree or not—guide people's behavior as much as, perhaps even more than, the 'harder' forms do. Among the most important of the intermediate kinds of belief is ideology.*"[14] From Higgs's definition, it's clear that one's political ideology is a highly personal belief, and it's equally clear why Hitler's[47] formulation[15] was effective and why Lenin's weapon of choice for fomenting social revolution was the brainwashing of children coupled with incessant propagandizing of the masses.

How Sociocommunism Became Entrenched in the US

To the total shock and surprise of many, the sociocommunist conspiracy in the US got seriously underway during the Woodrow Wilson administration—even before the October 1917 Revolution in Tsarist Russia. The impetus came from a surprising source: one Colonel Edward M. House[50] of Texas.[16]

---

[14]   *CRISIS AND LEVIATHAN*, 25th Anniversary Edition, by Robert Higgs, The Independent Institute, 2012, p. 36

[15]   "*The art of propaganda consists precisely in being able to awaken the imagination of the public through an appeal to their feelings.*" – Adolf Hitler, *MEIN KAMPF*

[16]   The following paragraph is taken from an Amazon.com book review of *PHILIP DRU, ADMINISTRATOR*[55]: "*Philip Dru: Administrator is a political fantasy novel about a military overthrow of the United States government and its Constitution. Its significance rests upon the fact that the novel represents the 'political and ethical faith' of the most influential presidential advisor in American History, Edward Mandell House. House was a close adviser to Presidents Woodrow Wilson and Franklin Roosevelt. Wilson called House his 'alter ego' and much of the economic program outlined in Dru can be found in Roosevelt's New Deal. It has been said that House 'copyrighted fascism' before Mussolini took power in Italy. House was not adverse to the allegation, writing in 1935 that he had 'anticipated Mussolini by several years' in the midst of an article which heaped praise upon Il Duce. Dru has had a greater impact on American government than the Communist Manifesto, Mein Kampf or any other tract of political extremism, yet by comparison, Dru is unknown. Philip Dru: Administrator belongs on the short shelf of any American interested in public affairs.*"

"In 1911, prior to Wilson's taking office as President, House had returned to his home in Texas and completed a book called PHILIP DRU, ADMINISTRATOR. Ostensibly a novel, it was actually a detailed plan for the future government of the United States, 'which would establish Socialism as dreamed by Karl Marx,' according to House. This 'novel' predicted the enactment of the graduated income tax, excess profits tax, unemployment insurance, social security and a flexible currency system. In short, it was the blueprint which was later followed by the Woodrow Wilson and Franklin D. Roosevelt[51] administrations."[17]

Students of sociocommunism well recognize that the primary cause of the statism disease is the supercilious conceit which gives rise to it. Possessed as they are of just such a supercilious conceit,[18] progressives (a.k.a. sociocommunists) are the principal reason that both the Democrat and Republican parties in the US continue to exhibit an irrepressible impulse to engage in the same kinds of social-engineering follies which have systematically devastated every country foolish enough to have statism thrust upon it. The "religious fervor" of early-twentieth-century sociocommunist missionaries, such as Colonel House and Woodrow Wilson—inspired as it was by the supercilious conceit of Francis Galton[52], the father of eugenics—is what motivated[53] Woodrow Wilson and his coterie of sycophantic Ivy League pseudointellectuals, and it continues unabated to this day.

The sociocommunist conspiracy in the US accelerated after World War I with the corrosive and subversive take-over of US teach-

---

[17] *SECRETS OF THE FEDERAL RESERVE (The London Connection)* by Eustace Mullins

[18] The following excerpt from Codevilla's "*America's Ruling Class – and the Perils of Revolution[56]*" is revealing. "*Its attitude is key to understanding our bipartisan ruling class. Its first tenet is that 'we' are the best and brightest while the rest of Americans are retrograde, racist and dysfunctional unless properly constrained. … As the 19th century ended, the educated class's religious fervor turned to social reform … Thus began the Progressive Era.*"

ers' colleges by sociocommunists. It gained strength during the Great Depression when many campus intellectuals—including the hapless J. Robert Oppenheimer[54]—were sufficiently disaffected with the evident failings of capitalism in the US that they unwittingly or wittingly associated with blatantly-open communists or communist-front organizations,[19] with many even becoming card-carrying members of the American Communist Party.[20] It accelerated again during the Vietnam War when Communist China brought a corrupting and debilitating drug culture to US college and university campuses.[21] And it became permanent in the 1970s when US educational institutions began conferring advanced degrees on antiwar activists as rewards for their countercultural animus, thereby ensur-

---

[19]   *"... the American Communist Party's own self-reporting actually claimed a higher number of members at its founding in 1919, when the American economy was doing just fine, contrasted with 1934, several painful years into the Great Depression,"* from the Introduction to *Red Herring: The Great Depression and the American Communist Party*[57] by Paul Kengor, Executive Director, the Center for Vision & Values at Grove City College, 2008

[20]   Although the subversive infiltration of Communists into US institutions and media was brought to light by Senator Joseph McCarthy[58] in the 1950s; McCarthyism ultimately failed to redress the situation because it failed to recognize the true nature of sociocommunism and the consequent need to break its insidious penetration of, and control over, US educational and governmental institutions in addition to domestic mass media.

[21]   From the earliest days of the Vietnam War, it was well known to the FBI that Communist China had deployed a small cadre of secret agents to the US to ply college and university campuses with free drugs, which they arranged to have shipped into the US via Mexico. That stratagem was undertaken by Communist China to undermine US support for the Vietnam War, as retribution for its defeat by the US in the Korean War, and as retribution for Chinese suffering at the hands of Occidentals in the infamous Opium Wars. The infiltration of Chinese Communist agents into US colleges and universities in the 1960s has never been officially acknowledged or exposed by the U.S. government. One can only speculate as to why it has not but, as in the case of the September 11, 2001 massacres, the failed U.S. government bureaucracies involved were greatly embarrassed by the ease with which a foreign enemy was able to infiltrate the US and violate its laws and, in the time-honored tradition of bureaucrats everywhere, rationalized that "what you don't know, won't hurt you" and covered it up to escape accountability.

ing that future generations would be subjected to a steady stream of Marxist-inspired ideology by faculties with no qualifying credentials other than their known sociocommunist sympathies.

UNDERSTANDING SOCIOCOMMUNISM

The Appeal of Sociocommunism

In spite of its many repeated and well-documented atrocities and catastrophic failures over the last one hundred years, sociocommunism continues to enjoy a seemingly irrepressible and universal appeal. The excerpt below provides a recognizably-correct and totally-satisfying explanation for that appeal.

> "*The incomparable success of Marxism* [in selling itself to the masses] *is due to the prospect it offers of fulfilling those dream aspirations and dreams of vengeance which have been so deeply embedded in the human soul from time immemorial. It promises a Paradise on earth, a Land of Heart's Desire full of happiness and enjoyment, and — sweeter still to the losers in life's game — humiliation of all who are stronger and better than the multitude.*" Taken from an English translation of the preface to the second German edition of *DIE GEMEINWIRTSCHAFT*[59] by Ludwig von Mises[60], January 1932

In fact, the false promises of sociocommunism are so appealing to the masses that most sociocommunists are not aware that it ultimately leads to fascism—i.e., in a direction opposite to one most would choose to go. Indeed, in most non-Muslim countries today, sociocommunism has become so imbued and inculcated in the masses from birth—through successive generations of brainwashing by sociocommunist demagogues and well-intentioned but woefully misguided and misled parents—that most of their citizens are not even aware they have become practicing sociocommunists. Sociocommunism is the sociopolitical culture into which they were born, and it's all they know.

Yet, no sane person—except those like Colonel House (if, indeed, he was sane), the infamous architect of the initial sociocommunist conspiracy in the US, who are infatuated with fascism and believe themselves to be ensconced in the ruling class—would knowingly choose to promote and support an ideology that inexorably leads to fascism.

Classical Sociocommunist Guerrilla-Warfare Tactics

When humans are forced by birthright or circumstances to eke out a subsistence-level lifestyle, and they are surrounded by others exhibiting opulent lifestyles, it's only natural for them to be envious and resentful. Thus, they will invariably become malcontented and easy prey for demagogues peddling sociocommunist agitprop—and more than a few will harbor "dream aspirations and dreams of vengeance" about escaping the ghetto and getting retribution for their unfortunate lot in life. When combined with the fact that humans, like all animals, will kill and steal to survive if necessary, it's easy to understand how the aggrieved can be persuaded that "ends justify the means" with no compunction whatever, why ghettos are rife with crime, and how the aggrieved can be readily exploited by sociocommunists to foment social revolution. It's not surprising then that the sociocommunist agenda is frequently disguised as a desire to improve the lot of aggrieved minorities. In reality, the sociocommunist agenda is to subjugate any such minorities on what Dinesh D'Souza[61] terms "urban plantations[62]," by providing them with so-called "welfare programs" designed to maintain them in subsistence-level lifestyles and permanent government dependency so they will become perpetual

reservoirs of malcontents duped into supporting their supposed bene-
factors while perpetually seeking retribution for their misfortune.

Indeed, exploitation of aggrieved minorities has been a primary
guerrilla-warfare tactic of sociocommunists from their inception and,
judging from their seeming indifference to the senseless decades-long
slaughter of innocents by criminal gangs and drug lords in US inner-
city ghettos—as exemplified by the abominable ongoing daily slaughter in today's Chicago ghettos—during nearly one hundred years
of maladministration by sociocommunists, it's fair to conclude that
sociocommunists have no more compassion for the downtrodden
than France's Louis XVI or Marie Antoinette did. Lyndon Johnson's[63]
"War on Poverty" is an instructive example. Supposedly designed to
lift aggrieved minorities out of poverty, US War on Poverty programs
have cost the US more than $22 trillion over more than fifty years
with no such effect, as noted in the excerpt below.

> *"Most of the Great Society was designed to fight
> LBJ's War on Poverty[64], the total cost of which has
> been the sum of $22 trillion in current [2014] dol-
> lars, as reckoned by the Heritage Foundation. The
> tally rises by about $1 trillion a year as more than
> 80 overlapping means-tested federal programs sap
> resources the country does not have. The $22 tril-
> lion figure is 'three times the amount of money that
> the government has spent on all military wars in
> its history, from the Revolutionary War to the pres-
> ent,' says Heritage's Robert Rector. ... What do we
> have to show for all this federal largesse? The pov-
> erty rate hasn't budged. Instead, we've seen the rise
> of multigenerational welfare dependency. For the $2
> trillion the federal government has spent on edu-
> cation since 1965, test scores have plummeted and
> the achievement gap between minority students and
> their peers has barely budged. Families, the bedrock
> of an authentically great society, have suffered most
> in LBJ's great social experiment. The overall out-of-
> wedlock birth rate has ballooned from 8 percent in*

*the mid-1960s to more than 40 percent today; from
25 percent to 73 percent among blacks."*

Harnessing the latent political power of aggrieved minorities
for the singular purpose of gaining and sustaining their own political
power is, and always has been, another primary guerrilla-warfare tactic of sociocommunists. It's why US sociocommunists want massive
numbers of unskilled immigrants. If immigrants are unskilled, they
are far more likely to wind up on an urban plantation where they can
be exploited for decades. And if the immigrants lack citizenship status and are not legally permitted to vote, resorting to their no-holds-
barred methods,[22] US globalist sociocommunists will do everything
in their power to grant them citizenship irrespective of the merits or
to encourage them to vote illegally.

Barack Obama is a prime example. Witness his many attempts
to violate US immigration laws and subvert the US Constitution
to facilitate mass importation of illegal immigrants. This in spite
of the fact that allegedly he is a constitutional scholar and—as evidenced by the following paragraph taken from President <u>George
Washington's</u>[65] <u>1796 Farewell Address</u>[66]—the US was well warned
from its inception about the dangers of one branch of its government
usurping the powers of another.

> *"It is important, likewise, that the habits of think-
> ing in a free country should inspire caution in
> those entrusted with its administration, to confine
> themselves within their respective constitutional
> spheres, avoiding in the exercise of the powers of one
> department to encroach upon another. The spirit of*

---

[22] *"The communists must be prepared to make every sacrifice and, if necessary, even
resort to all sorts of cunning schemes and stratagems, to employ illegal methods, to
evade and conceal the truth ... The practical part of <u>communist policy</u>[67] is to incite
one against another ... My words were calculated to evoke hatred, aversion, and
contempt ... not to convince but to break up the ranks of the opponent, not to correct
an opponent's mistake but to destroy him, to wipe his organization off the face of the
earth. This formulation is indeed of such a nature as to evoke the worst thoughts,
the worst suspicions about the opponent." –* Vladimir Ilyich Ulyanov, aka Lenin

encroachment tends to consolidate the powers of all the departments in one, and thus to create, whatever the form of government, a real despotism. A just estimate of that love of power, and proneness to abuse it, which predominates in the human heart, is sufficient to satisfy us of the truth of this position. The necessity of reciprocal checks in the exercise of political power, by dividing and distributing it into different depositaries, and constituting each the guardian of the public weal against invasions by the others, has been evinced by experiments ancient and modern; some of them in our country and under our own eyes. To preserve them must be as necessary as to institute them. If, in the opinion of the people, the distribution or modification of the constitutional powers be in any particular wrong, let it be corrected by an amendment in the way which the Constitution designates. But let there be no change by usurpation; for though this, in one instance, may be the instrument of good, it is the customary weapon by which free governments are destroyed. The precedent must always greatly overbalance in permanent evil any partial or transient benefit, which the use can at any time yield."

Yet, as demonstrated by the Barack Obama administration, George Washington's prescient warning has fallen on deaf ears or is being deliberately ignored. That is not to say the US Constitution is perfect. It's not. If the framers of the US Constitution had Mencken's premonition,[23] they surely would not have put one person in charge of US foreign policy. The legacy of the Jimmy Carter administration stands as incontrovertible testimony to their error. By refusing to support the Shah of Iran and thereby facilitating the 1979 Islamic revolution—the primary achievement of which has been perfection of the world's most heinous terrorist weapon, namely: mass murder via homicide bombers—Carter was complicit in unleashing homicide bombers on the world. That single act of not supporting the Shah of Iran destabilized the Middle East for more than forty years and launched a decades-long explosion of radical Islamic terrorism that has since murdered millions of innocents and continues to spread largely unabated throughout the Muslim world.

Like Machiavelli[68], Marx, Lenin, and Alinsky[69] before them, all contemporary sociocommunists believe "ends justify the means," and consequently, they don't hesitate to employ any means necessary to achieve their goals. Its no-holds-barred methods are another way in which sociocommunism distinguishes itself from other political and economic theories as exceptionally evil, lethal, and pernicious. Armed with missionary hubris and zeal, which can only be derived from profound arrogance and ignorance, sociocommunist revolutionaries don't hesitate to commit heinous crimes to achieve their agenda. Thus, they have no compunction whatever about promulgating the most outrageous lies,[24] and—recognizing that revolutionary zeal is greatly enhanced during a crisis—they don't hesitate to

---

[23]   *"The larger the mob, the harder the test. In small areas, before small electorates, a first-rate man occasionally fights his way through, carrying even the mob with him by force of his personality. But when the field is nationwide, and the fight must be waged chiefly at second and third hand, and the force of personality cannot so readily make itself felt, then all the odds are on the man who is, intrinsically, the most devious and mediocre – the man who can most easily adeptly disperse the notion that his mind is a virtual vacuum. ... The Presidency tends, year by year, to go to such men. As democracy is perfected, the office represents, more and more closely, the inner soul of the people. We move toward a lofty ideal. On some great and glorious day the plain folks of the land will reach their heart's desire at last, and the White House will be adorned by a downright moron." –* H. L. Mencken[74]

[24]   Recent research confirms that a liar's propensity to lie actually increases over time.

contrive a crisis du jour that can be effectively exploited through cunningly-designed agitprop whenever the need arises—with anthropomorphic global warming only one of their more-successful frauds[70].

Ever since Lenin's success in overthrowing the Russian Tsarist regime, all sociocommunist demagogues have become enthusiastic practitioners of the "Big Lie"—knowing, as did Marx, Lenin, and Hitler, that the bigger the lie the easier it is to sell to the masses.[25] Indeed, through exploitation of modern mass media, promulgation of the "Big Lie" is now the most powerful guerrilla-warfare tactic in the sociocommunist repertoire. So effective has it been that deliberate deception spread through outrageous lies is now the most-popular sociocommunist guerrilla-warfare tactic as well, and in the US today, most sociocommunist agitprop is masked under the euphemism of political correctness.

Interestingly, President Woodrow Wilson's Committee for Public Information[71], created seven days after the US entered World War I in 1917 as a means of garnering support for his highly unpopular entry into the war, was the first to use modern audiovisual mass media[72]—in the form of officially-produced government newsreels[26]—as a means of disseminating political agitprop. Indeed, his Committee for Public Information was so successful that it became the blueprint for Hitler's own Ministry for Popular Enlightenment and Propaganda[73]. Like Wilson, Hitler soon recognized the power of modern audiovisual mass media as an instrument for shaping political ideologies.[27]

A Political and Economic Theory Built on Quicksand

---

[25] *"A lie told often enough becomes the truth."* – Vladimir Ilyich Ulyanov, aka Lenin

[26] When the US entered World War I, the Committee for Public Information began producing its own newsreels entitled the Official War Review.

[27] *"It was during the War* [World War I]*, however, that we had the best chance of estimating the tremendous results which could be obtained by a propagandist system properly carried out. ... I had ample opportunity to learn a practical lesson in this matter; for, unfortunately, it was only too well taught us by the enemy."* – Adolf Hitler, *MEIN KAMPF*

Perhaps Ludwig von Mises was aided by the fact that he was born (two years before Marx died) into the same society known to Marx. Whatever the case, his indictment of Marx is at once recognizably correct, totally satisfying, and absolutely devastating. The English translation[75] of the preface to the second German edition of *DIE GEMEINWIRTSCHAFT* cited earlier contains the following:

> "*It was at this moment that Marx appeared. Adept as he was in Hegelian dialectic – a system easy of abuse by those who seek to dominate thought by arbitrary flights of fancy and metaphysical verbosity – he was not slow in finding a way out of the dilemma in which socialists found themselves. Since Science and Logic had argued against Socialism, it was imperative to devise a system which could be relied on to defend it against such unpalatable criticism. This was the task which Marxism undertook to perform. It had three lines of procedure. First, it denied that Logic is universally valid for all mankind and for all ages. Thought, it stated, was determined by the class of the thinkers; was in fact an 'ideological superstructure' of their class interests. The type of reasoning which had refuted the socialist idea was 'revealed' as 'bourgeois' reasoning, an apology for Capitalism. Secondly, it laid it down that the dialectical development led of necessity to Socialism; that the aim and end of all history was the socialization of the means of production by the expropriation of the expropriators – the negation of negation. Finally, it was ruled that no one should be allowed to put forward, as the Utopians had done, any definite proposals for the construction of the Socialist Promised Land. Since the coming of Socialism was inevitable, Science would best renounce all attempts to determine its nature. ... Logic and reasoning, which might show the absurdity of such dreams of bliss and revenge, are to be thrust aside. Marxism*

is thus the most radical of all reactions against the reign of scientific thought over life and action, established by Rationalism. It is against Logic, against Science and against the activity of thought itself – its outstanding principle is the prohibition of thought and inquiry, especially as applied to the institutions and workings of a socialist economy. ... The Bolshevists persistently tell us that religion is opium for the people. Marxism is indeed opium for those who might take to thinking and must therefore be weaned from it."

There can be absolutely no doubt that political correctness is based on the same kinds of sophisms as those which are the basis for Marxism. Similarly, as is evident from the following excerpts, even those with reading comprehension no greater than that of a third-grader will quickly recognize the Marxism-inspired sophisms underpinning what are now termed "postmodernist relativism," "postmodernism[76]," and "radical relativism."

"Eschewing any reference to truths of this kind, adherents of postmodernist relativism assess morality instead by the sole criterion of power: Those without it deserve the ethical high ground by virtue of their very status as underdogs; those with it, at least if they are Westerners, and especially if they are Americans, are ipso facto oppressors." 'Bomb Texas,' The psychological roots of anti-Americanism[77], Victor Davis Hanson, *The Wall Street Journal* Editorial Page, January 13, 2003

"We are finally reaping the rewards of postmodernism. Thirty years of radical relativism propagated by my addled and destructive generation [The author is seemingly unaware that this pernicious political movement was well underway in the U.S. in the 1920s and 1930s.] *in the universities, seemingly unchallenged by parents or university*

regents adds up to this: People believe that there is no objective truth. Truth has become something to be invented, rather than pursued. Reasoned argument is a tool of white males so has no value. If you feel it, only then can it be true." <u>Radical relativism and the war in Iraq</u>[78], Elizabeth Nickson, National Post, April 5, 2003

At a time when the <u>WSJ reports</u>[79] that *"About a third of Americans ages 18-29 support socialism, while not even half back capitalism"* and when US college and university campuses have become centers for organized protests against anything and everything objectionable to globalist sociocommunists, one gets a measure of just how far the US has "progressed" down the slippery slope of sociocommunism. To any objective observer with a historical perspective, it's transparently obvious that the US has allowed a long-simmering caldron of socio-communist activists, agitators, and their sympathizers to stealthily and systematically corrupt and take over its educational and governmental institutions. In so doing, it has enabled sociocommunist ideologues to implement Lenin's weapon of choice for fomenting social revolution, namely: the brainwashing of children and incessant propagandizing of the masses.

As the human brain is not fully developed prior to age twenty-five, children are ill-equipped to resist brainwashing disguised as education—especially when that "education" seemingly has the approval of both parents and guardians. Thus, the brainwashing of children is little different from the Skinnerian conditioning of laboratory animals. And as one's political ideology is a highly-personal belief that is easily swayed by cunningly-designed agitprop, the awful reality is that—through five generations of indoctrination with sociocommunist agitprop—the US has allowed its so-called "educational institutions" to produce generations of US citizens with sociocommunist sympathies. Indeed, US grammar schools and high schools have become little more than poorly-managed unsupervised day-care centers functioning as <u>sociocommunist reeducation camps</u>[80]—similar to the "reeducation through labor" camps established during the Cultural Revolution in Communist China—for expunging all historical, parental, and religious influences while radicalizing students by indoctrinating them with globalist sociocommunist agitprop in the guise of education. Similarly, US colleges and universities have become centers for producing new generations of globalist sociocommunist activists. As a consequence, the US—which once ranked first in the world[81]—now ranks fourteenth out of forty[82] industrialized countries in education, and US educational standards have declined so much over the last one hundred years that they have become an international embarrassment.

Another consequence of the failure of US educational institutions is that modern media in the US have become so effectively brainwashed by globalist sociocommunist agitprop and have such a poor command of the English language that they are unable to distinguish between the innocuous and the purposely deceitful. Taking their cue from Lenin,[28] sociocommunists never fail to try to hide their true intentions and meaning through the deliberate abuse of language. Thus, current discourse in the US is replete with deliberately-misleading politically-correct euphemisms, such as: "democratic" instead of "democrat"; "diversity" instead of "multiculturalism"[29]; "educated" instead of "brainwashed" or "indoctrinated"; "global warming" instead of "natural climate change"; "leading from behind" instead of "following" or "refusing to lead"; "leftist" or "liberal" or "progressive" or "secular progressive" instead of "sociocommunist"; "politically correct" instead of "politically contrived"; "politically correct speech" instead of "political agitprop"; "radical" instead of "seditious"; "suspect" instead of "assailant" or "perpetrator"; etc., ad nauseam.

Sadly, many contemporary Europeans appear to have learned precisely nothing from the catastrophic events of twentieth-century European history. Fortunately, there are some who, having thoroughly studied communism, well recognize its inherent evils.

---

[28]   "*First confuse the vocabulary.*" – Vladimir Ilyich Ulyanov, aka Lenin

[29]   "*The lie behind the buzzword of diversity could not be made more clear. If you don't conform, then you don't count as diverse, no matter what your personal background.*" – Peter Andreas Thiel, as reported in "What Trump represents isn't crazy, and it's not going away," *USA Today*[87], 31 October 2016

Anthony A. M. Daniels, a.k.a. <u>Theodore Dalrymple</u>[83], is one such individual as evidenced by the following:

> "<u>*Political correctness*</u>[84] *is communist propaganda writ small. In my study of communist societies, I came to the conclusion that the purpose of communist propaganda was not to persuade or convince, not to inform, but to humiliate; and therefore, the less it corresponded to reality the better. When people are forced to remain silent when they are being told the most obvious lies, or even worse when they are forced to repeat the lies themselves, they lose once and for all their sense of probity. To assent to obvious lies is to cooperate with evil, and in some small way to become evil oneself. One's standing to resist anything is thus eroded, and even destroyed. A society of emasculated liars is easy to control. I think if you examine political correctness, it has the same effect and is intended to.*"

In this light, political correctness is seen to be nothing more nor less than a sociocommunist cover for Lenin's policy of deliberate dissimulation for the purpose of fomenting social revolution. <u>Ronald Reagan</u>[85] was correct, sociocommunism <u>is inherently evil</u>[86], as its modus operandi is to promulgate fiendishly-contrived disinformation which exploits innate human weaknesses to instigate social revolutions which inexorably lead to enslavement of the masses and enormous human suffering.

The renouncing of logic and science by sociocommunists so eloquently documented by von Mises has myriad pernicious societal impacts. Chief among them is its tragic encouragement of the ignorant to forecast outcomes and remedies for phenomena and processes for which there is insufficient scientific knowledge on which to base any such forecasts with a respectable degree of confidence. Sadly, humans have a most unfortunate propensity, namely: a willingness to plunge ahead with half-baked remedies based on the flimsiest of evidence of their actual efficacy before acquiring a prudent understanding of a problem, or its potential causes, or the potential unintended consequences which could result from applications of their nostrums.

Alas, like medieval clerics threatening people with damnation and hellfire from their pulpits, modern fear-mongers—such as 350.org[88], Al Gore[89], Bill McKibben[90], Green Peace[91], James E. Hansen[92], Sierra Club[93], and assorted other self-appointed "keepers of the faith"—derive huge financial benefits from such scare tactics. What is worse is that, by potentially wreaking havoc with both local and global economies, such scoundrels—presuming to have solutions to real or imagined problems with neither the problems nor the solutions well-defined or substantiated by respectable scientific evidence—could well add to human suffering and cause adverse consequences far worse than any they presume to ameliorate. Witness people needlessly starving simply because the European Union—in an effort to protect its markets from competition with US produce—cast a dark cloud over genetically-modified foods, thus persuading ignorant leaders in less-affluent and less-developed nations to embargo genetically-modified foods as well.

While medieval clerics threatening damnation and hellfire were on safe ground, as their theses could not be scientifically refuted, the same is not true of the modern fear-mongers. Most of the lies of modern fear-mongers are based on simple greed, ignorance, or malice and are quickly refuted when subjected to coldly-objective scientific scrutiny. Suffice to say, the most ignorant and most venal members of society are not to be trusted with their prescriptions for salvation of the human species. That is not to say the US wasn't well warned about the potentially corrosive and corrupting influence of government funding on scientific research. Indeed, the danger was highlighted by none other than President Dwight D. Eisenhower[94] in his 17 January 1961 Farewell Address to the Nation[95], excerpted immediately below.

"In the councils of government, we must guard against the acquisition of unwarranted influence, whether sought or unsought, by the military-industrial complex. The potential for the disastrous rise of misplaced

power exists and will persist. We must never let the weight of this combination endanger our liberties or democratic processes. We should take nothing for granted. Only an alert and knowledgeable citizenry can compel the proper meshing of the huge industrial and military machinery of defense with our peaceful methods and goals, so that security and liberty may prosper together. Akin to, and largely responsible for the sweeping changes in our industrial-military posture, has been the technological revolution during recent decades. In this revolution, research has become central; it also becomes more formalized, complex, and costly. A steadily increasing share is conducted for, by, or at the direction of, the Federal government. Today, the solitary inventor, tinkering in his shop, has been overshadowed by task forces of scientists in laboratories and testing fields. In the same fashion, the free university, historically the fountainhead of free ideas and scientific discovery, has experienced a revolution in the conduct of research. Partly because of the huge costs involved, a government contract becomes virtually a substitute for intellectual curiosity. For every old blackboard there are now hundreds of new electronic computers. The prospect of domination of the nation's scholars by Federal employment, project allocations, and the power of money is ever present – and is gravely to be regarded. Yet, in holding scientific research and discovery in respect, as we should, we must also be alert to the equal and opposite danger that public policy could itself become the captive of a scientific-technological elite."

Unsurprisingly, the cozy relationship between the US government and private industry dates back to the infamous Woodrow Wilson administration and his creation of a <u>War Industries Board</u>[96] in July 1917. That relationship blossomed to a much greater extent during World War II and undoubtedly is what prompted Eisenhower's prescient warning.

WHY PEOPLE ARE VULNERABLE TO SOCIOCOMMUNIST LIES

Innate Animalism and Human Weakness

There is every reason to believe that the framers of the US Constitution were well aware of <u>Alexander Tytler</u>'s[30] [97]indictment that all democracies are doomed, to wit:

> "[Democracy is] *nothing better than an Utopian theory, a splendid chimera, descriptive of a state of society that never did, and never could exist; a republic not of men, but of angels. … While man is being instigated by the love of power – a passion visible in an infant, and common to us even with the inferior animals – he will seek personal superiority in preference to every matter of a general concern; or at best, he will employ himself in advancing the public good, as the means of individual distinction and elevation: he will promote the interest of the state from the selfish but most useful passion of making himself considerable in that establishment*

---

30   Alexander Fraser Tytler, aka Lord Woodhouselee (10/15/1747–1/5/1813)

which he labors to aggrandize. Such is the true pic-
ture of man as a political agent."[31]

Note that if Tytler's indictment of democracy is correct, then democracy and sociocommunism have the same seductive appeal to the same innate human weaknesses—which collectively hold out the tantalizing prospect of a free ride at someone else's expense. Thus, it's indelibly clear why democracies provide fertile ground for sociocommunism and why European socialistic democracies are so enamored of it.[32] Moreover, if Tytler's indictment is correct, then sociocommunism surely will accelerate the demise of any democracy.

While Tytler's insight is instructive, it leaves unanswered the question of what it is about human nature that makes democracy and sociocommunism so insidious and seductive. With the benefit of more than two hundred years of additional sociopolitical experience, it's now evident that what makes people vulnerable to false hopes for democracy and sociocommunism is an inability, in the absence of prior pertinent experience, to perceive and fully appreciate the

---

[31] *UNIVERSAL HISTORY[99] (from the Creation of the World to the Beginning of the Eighteenth Century)* by Alexander Fraser Tytler, Volume I, Hilliard, Gray & Company, 1839

[32] *"The Europeans have created a vast constellation of domestic policy interventions that are cloaked in the seductive rhetoric of compassion, fairness and cultural sophistication. These policies include highly generous welfare benefits for the unemployed; state ownership and subsidy of key industries (such as Airbus); rules that make it difficult to hire and fire workers; prohibitions against closing down plants; heavy protections of labor unions against competitive forces; mandatory worker benefit packages that include health insurance, child care allowances, paid parental leave, four to six weeks of vacation; shortened work weeks; and, alas, high taxes on business and labor to pay for these lavish benefits. ... In [the U.S.] Congress today there is some bill to provide virtually every social welfare benefit that Europe now offers. ... Europe is now paying a high price for this failed experiment with welfare state socialism. Today's populist revolt against economic integration in France and Germany suggests that these nations remain mysteriously impervious to the need for change. A bigger mystery is why some American politicians are so intent on repeating Europe's mistakes." – The European Disease, Economic anxiety is a product of the welfare state,* 3 June 2005

dangers and folly inherent in pursuing unachievable dreams and fantasies.

Alas, the inability to perceive and fully appreciate such dangers and folly results from other more basic human weaknesses, namely: human greed coupled with a penchant for self-indulgence, an inability to reliably distinguish between fantasies and realities, and a propensity to plunge ahead without fully analyzing potential unintended consequences. Thus, there is no mystery as to why history is strewn with failed sociopolitical experiments—most of which have had disastrous, if not monstrous, consequences. What is the source of these unfortunate human characteristics? It's nothing more nor less than the innate animalism of the human species.

As people age, most of them lose their innate innocence, naiveté, and its consequent youthful idealism as surely as they lose their virginity, but it's not instantaneous. It's part of a natural maturation process. This phenomenon comports well with much empirical evidence of a gradually increasing economic and political conservatism as a natural part of the human aging process. As succinctly stated by Winston Churchill[98], "*If you are young and not liberal, then you have no heart; but if you are old and not conservative, then you have no brain.*" The entire process can be summed up by the aphorism: "*Too soon old and too late smart.*"

Sadly, a significant portion of the human population fails to achieve full mental maturity and remains in a child-like state of mental immaturity, some even into senescence, due to what some might term "the curse of the big brain"—i.e., a frequent inability to distinguish between fantasies and realities. It takes a disciplined mind that has been previously exposed to harsh realities to distinguish between the two—and it's an all-too-common phenomenon to find otherwise-intelligent individuals completely lacking in that ability. Alas, with the advent of augmented-realty and virtual-reality systems, distinguishing between fantasy and reality is surely going to become an even greater challenge in the future.

In any case, the perceptions of immature humans already are encumbered by a whole host of problems stemming from their innate animalism, not the least of which are an insatiable appetite for constant mental stimulation and titillation; a consequent near-universal addiction to anything that will provide amusement; an ability to conjure images never seen and imagine events that never occurred with equal clarity and memorability to those actually experienced; an ability to indulge in comforting fantasies while denying or ignoring harsh realities; and an ability to individually and collectively shut out realities while deceiving themselves and others.

In this regard, Chris Argyris's[100] maturity theory[101], as summarized immediately below, is particularly germane.

> *"According to Argyris, seven changes should take place in the personality of individuals if they are to develop into mature people over the years.*
> — *First, individuals move from a passive state as infants to a state of increasing activity as adults.*
> — *Second, individuals develop from a state of dependence upon others as infants to a state of relative independence as adults.*
> — *Third, individuals behave in only a few ways as infants, but as adults they are capable of behaving in many ways.*
> — *Fourth, individuals have erratic, casual and shallow interests as infants but develop deeper and stronger interests as adults.*
> — *Fifth, the time perspective of children is very short, involving only the present, but as they mature, their time perspective increases to include the past and the future.*
> — *Sixth, individuals as infants are subordinate to everyone, but they move to equal or superior positions with others as adults.*
> — *Seventh, as children, individuals lack an awareness of 'self,' but as adults they are not only aware of, but they are able to control 'self.'*

> *Argyris postulates that these changes reside on a continuum and that the 'healthy' personality develops from 'immaturity' to 'maturity.' ... These changes are only general tendencies, but they give some light on the matter of maturity. Norms of the individual's culture and personality inhibit and limit maximum expression and growth of the adult, yet the tendency is to move toward the 'maturity' end of the continuum with age. ... Argyris would be the first to admit that few, if any, develop to full maturity."*

Retardation of the natural maturation process neatly accounts for the egregious naiveté that is a fundamental part of sociocommunist personalities. Sociocommunists invariably exhibit an egregious lack of maturation in the second, fifth, and seventh stages of Argyris's model of the human maturation process. If one is infantile, it's natural to project infantile dependence on everyone else; and that is why sociocommunists universally believe the masses are incapable of caring for themselves without government intervention. Similarly, if one is preoccupied with the present (the "now" generations), then one surely will not assimilate the lessons of history or potential vagaries of the future. Add to that insistence on immediate self-gratification and a complete inability to exercise self-control and self-restraint (the "me" generations) engendered by the teachings of Benjamin Spock[102], and you have the retarded personality development of today's archetype sociocommunist.

Thus, it's not surprising sociocommunists take themselves so seriously and exhibit an infantile lack of self-perspective or a sense of humor. When one takes oneself as seriously as do infants, it's not possible to view oneself as others might, nor is it possible to find the contradictions and humor in one's own infantile fumblings and musings. It's no mystery why adolescents are universally known to overestimate their limited knowledge of complex phenomena so succinctly captured in the term "terrible teens."

Nowhere is that phenomenon more in evidence than in infantile understandings of economics, politics, and world history, and it makes immature personalities particularly vulnerable to the false promises and sophisms of Marxism, the seductive appeal of socio-communism, and the ravings of demagogues and fear-mongers of every stripe.

It's no coincidence that few social revolutions succeed without the active support of adolescents. That reality was well understood by both Lenin and Hitler, as demonstrated by their formation of the Young Communist League[103] and Nazi Youth League[104], respectively, and it is being exploited today by the deep penetration of globalist sociocommunist activists, agitators, and their sympathizers into US educational institutions, as well as by seditious organizations like La Raza[105] operating on the campuses of US colleges and universities.

The Natural and Unavoidable Consequences of Organization

People are not born with an innate understanding of management and organization, yet precious little of significance can be accomplished by people in their absence. Consequently, the skills needed to build and manage successful organizations must be learned. Unfortunately, the needed skills can't be effectively taught by academics with no firsthand experience in building organizations. That unfortunate reality explains why MBA programs are no substitute for actual business experience, and it also explains the dreadful mismanagement of educational and governmental institutions, the majority of which are mismanaged by executives with little or no prior business experience.

It also serves as a healthy reminder of why trust in academics and so-called "experts" is frequently misplaced. While there is some truth to John Maynard Keynes's[106] observation that:

> "... the ideas of economists and political philosophers, both when they are right and when they are wrong, are more powerful than is commonly understood. Indeed the world is ruled by little else. Practical men, who believe themselves to be quite

exempt from any intellectual influences, are usually the slaves of some defunct economist. Madmen in authority, who hear voices in the air, are distilling their frenzy from some academic scribbler of a few years back. I am sure that the power of vested interests is vastly exaggerated compared with the gradual encroachment of ideas." THE GENERAL THEORY OF EMPLOYMENT, INTEREST AND MONEY[107] by John Maynard Keynes, 1936, Chapter 24, pp. 383-384

It's also true that knowledge does not automatically grant wisdom. Merriam-Webster's Unabridged Dictionary defines "wisdom" as "the intelligent application of learning," thereby making an important distinction between knowledge and its intelligent application. Were it not so, academicians might well have the answers to all of life's important questions. Unfortunately, they do not, and their acquisition of wisdom is greatly impeded by the cloistering provided by educational and governmental institutions in which executives and employees are insulated from many of the real-world challenges and realities faced by ordinary citizens.

As many important questions that should be of life-and-death concern to every human go unaddressed or unanswered, examples abound. For a species that prides itself on its superior intelligence and wisdom, one might well pose the following questions:

- How wise is a species that allows state sponsors of genocide and terror to acquire weapons of mass destruction?
- How wise is a species that is aware there is a nonzero probability that most, if not all, animal life on earth can be wiped out by the impact of a single asteroid[108], which could occur at any time without warning, yet—even when it has the means to do so—makes no plan to establish a colony on the moon[109] which might ensure it could survive such an eventuality?
- How wise is a species that knows it treats what it deems to be less-intelligent earthly life-forms either as food, pests,

or pets, yet deludes itself into believing that any <u>intelligent</u> <u>extraterrestrial</u>[110] life-forms it might encounter anywhere in the universe will be capable of only benign behavior and will pose no threat to itself?

"I'd rather entrust the government of the United States to the first 400 people listed in the Boston telephone directory than to the faculty of Harvard University." <u>William F. Buckley, Jr.</u>[111]

Building and managing successful organizations of any kind is no mean feat, and human history is filled with countless examples of organizational failures, most of which are due to the same human politics that are responsible for the failures of democracy and socio-communism. Like all politics, the politics afflicting organizations are an inevitable consequence of human nature, and—as human nature does not change quickly—there is every reason to believe such failures will continue indefinitely.

As all organizations exist to manage human endeavors requiring the efforts of more than one person, they all require apportionment of the total requisite effort into smaller efforts that can be allocated to, and executed by, individuals. In general, the smaller efforts are not independent of each other, so an additional management effort is required to coordinate the smaller efforts. If the management effort by itself requires the efforts of more than one person, then it must be similarly apportioned; and to function effectively, the resulting management team must have a chain of command to maintain control and to hold subordinates accountable for their allocated portions of the effort.

Thus, every management team has an inescapable need for a hierarchy of authorities and responsibilities. If its management hierarchy breaks down, the effectivity and efficiency of the entire organization will suffer as clearly-communicated and well-defined objectives, as well as disciplined accountability for achieving them, are needed at every level. In the absence of such clearly-communicated and well-defined objectives and/or disciplined accountability, all organizations naturally evolve into bloated, mindless, self-aggrandizing, self-perpetuating, self-righteous, self-serving, and unaccountable bureaucracies lacking competence, direction, and purpose.

Sadly, nothing kills with more impunity than that kind of mindless bureaucracy, and its culpable members can, and frequently do, escape punishment for even the most heinous crimes. The following two tragic examples will suffice to illustrate the kinds of atrocities that can, and do, result from mindless bureaucracy, namely: the National Weather Service bureaucrat who ignored Cuba's warnings of the 1900 category-four Galveston hurricane and was therefore directly responsible for six-thousand-plus fatalities was promoted; and the officials who ignored repeated warnings from the designers of the launch vehicle—including NASA's own engineers—of the possibility of O-ring failures due to freezing temperatures during the launch of the Challenger space shuttle, and therefore, were directly responsible for willfully killing all seven members of its crew, were never held accountable.

In his study of the sociology of political-party organizations, Robert Michels[112] observed an Iron Law of Oligarchy[113], which he outlined as follows:

> "*The fundamental sociological law of political parties (the term 'political' being here used in its most comprehensive sense) may be formulated in the following terms: 'It is organization which gives birth to the domination of the elected over the electors, of the mandataries over the mandators, of the delegates over the delegators. Who says organization, says oligarchy.*"

Merriam-Webster's Unabridged Dictionary defines "politics" as "competition between competing interest groups or individuals for power and leadership." As individual authorities and responsibilities increase from lower levels to higher levels in any management hierarchy, every such hierarchy naturally breeds competition among the members of the organization it controls. Accordingly, Michels's observation might as well be termed the "Iron Law of Organization," as it applies equally well to all organizations. Thus, as a direct consequence of basic human nature and competition, internal infighting and politics—which are the bane of any organization—will be found in organizations of every kind.

Frequently described as a contact sport, if we accept Tytler's "true picture of man as a political agent," politics might better be described as a blood sport with no rules. As such, it's a game in which competitors will use any means to win, with tactics ranging from harmless deception to outright assassination.[33] That is why "politics" is always "personal," "political" is a synonym for "possibly disingenuous," and "political gentility" is, and always will be, an oxymoron.

The inevitability of no-holds-barred politics is a direct consequence of unsuppressed human cupidity and corruptibility, the inevitability of ongoing political wars between factions, and the natural escalation of political warfare as stakes become greater and political factions become ever more polarized. That is especially true of the partisan politics between political parties.

The Natural and Unavoidable Consequences of Government

As every government is comprised of one or more organizations, all of the natural and unavoidable consequences of organization apply equally to government. Consequently, if a government permits its employees to form labor unions and/or institutes so-called "civil service" laws, which protect them from disciplined accountability, then it's committing inexorable suicide as its organizations will naturally evolve into bloated, mindless, self-aggrandizing, self-perpetuating, self-righteous, self-serving, and unaccountable bureaucracies lacking competence, direction, and purpose.

Police, policy, and polity all derive from the ancient Greek and Latin[114] words for government or state. Thus, from the very beginnings of civic government, laws have been convolved with law

---

[33]   *"There are no morals in politics; there is only expedience. A scoundrel may be of use to us just because he is a scoundrel."* – Vladimir Ilyich Ulyanov, aka Lenin

enforcement, and it was implicitly understood that every additional law or regulation would deprive the governed of additional liberties they would otherwise enjoy. Even the ancient Greeks understood that governmental tyranny ineluctably increases with each and every additional law or regulation imposed on the governed.

Unfortunately, government implies oversight, and oversight naturally gives rise to a perceived sense of entitlement among the overseers. What is worse is that this sense of entitlement especially appeals to, and attracts, those who wish to "lord it over" others like feudal overlords, and—in combination with unaccountability and unassailable job security—the overseers naturally begin to perceive themselves to be members of a separate ruling class. As a separate ruling-class mentality takes hold, it naturally leads to progressively more autocratic and self-serving government, which inevitably leads to plundering of the nation's treasury. When added to the travesties of unaccountability and unassailable job security, these factors inexorably give rise to the kinds of cronyism, incompetence, and nepotism found in government bureaucracies large and small as they become increasingly autocratic and self-serving.

The tendency of governments to become increasingly autocratic is especially pernicious and virulent when governed by "outsiders"—i.e., by bureaucrats who perceive themselves to be different from the governed. That is why government by outsiders inevitably leads to enslavement of the governed and why self-government is the only form of government that the governed, given a choice, will tolerate indefinitely. Even if one had a naively benign view of governmental overreach and power, when combined with a realistic awareness that there is nothing as fearsome or loathsome as bloated, mindless, self-aggrandizing, self-perpetuating, self-righteous, self-serving, and unaccountable government bureaucracies marching to the beats of their own drummers, it's enough to strike terror in the hearts of even the bravest souls.

The reduction in freedoms enjoyed by the governed as government places increasing constraints on individual behaviors inevitably leads to some homogenization of the governed. However, if globalist sociocommunist theories of multiculturalism weaken such homogenization to the point that the governed have no more in common with each other than a set of laws, the government becomes highly unstable and is subject to collapse due to potential Balkanization of its citizens into factions with no strong bonds holding them together.

It's worth noting that the globalist sociocommunist stratagem to bring about Balkanization and disintegration of the US through open borders has many precedents, as the suicidal folly of multiculturalism has been repeated throughout human history. The former Soviet Union provides a recent example. Even though it tried valiantly for nearly seventy years to homogenize its citizens with its Russification[115] process, it was unable to suppress the use of more than one hundred different languages[116] and utterly failed to establish enough of a common culture to prevent its eventual Balkanization and disintegration.

Indeed, no empire which ever attempted to span a large number of different cultures—not those of Alexander the Great, the ancient Romans, Genghis Khan, Charlemagne, Saladin, Tamerlane, Napoleon, the Ottomans, Portugal, Spain, Great Britain, the Third Reich, the Soviet Union, nor any other—has ever succeeded in bridging the chasms which separate peoples of different cultures, despite the fact that most bankrupted themselves in failed attempts to do so. The ancient Romans never learned that lesson though it had ample opportunities to do so, nor it seems have the Europeans who are now attempting to forge a united nation from a loose aggregation of tribes which have been warring with each other for two thousand years. Good luck to them; they surely will need it.

In many ways, the decadence and sloth of the citizens of ancient Rome, having achieved a previously unprecedented affluence, were precursors of the social debilities presently afflicting US citizens. Indeed, Roman citizens were so accustomed to the idle sloth of their pampered existence, they could not even raise an effective military to defend themselves against barbarian invasions; and they repeatedly made the same mistake of importing, enslaving, and training barbarians—Goths, Vandals, Angles, Saxons, Lombards, Suebi, Frisii, Jutes, Franks, Huns, Avars, Slavs, and Bulgars—to do their fighting for them. Unfortunately for them, once equipped with superior

Roman military equipment and trained in Roman military tactics, many of the barbarians chose to stay to enjoy the more-affluent lifestyles of the Romans—with the predictable result that Balkanization eventually led to the complete disintegration of the Roman Empire.

In stark contrast, the US has been unique in its ability to successfully absorb and integrate peoples from many diverse cultural backgrounds—and the only thing which has made that possible until recently has been assimilation of foreign-born citizens through insistence on their acceptance of English as the single official US language and their sworn allegiance to the US Constitution. That singular achievement is now threatened by counterproductive laws based on infantile ignorance of human nature and its derivative globalist sociocommunist theories of multiculturalism. When examined objectively, it's clear that multiculturalism has been a cause of much of the world's strife, and that the globalist sociocommunist "diversity" farce inevitably leads to Balkanization, political unrest, and social discord.

THE INSIDIOUS SOCIOCOMMUNIST REVOLUTIONARY PROCESS

Acquire Local Political Power through Unionization

US labor unions have provided fertile ground for the spread of sociocommunism for more than one hundred years. For decades in the first half of the twentieth century, blue-collar unions were an active source of sociocommunist recruitment and training, as well as a powerful source of sociocommunist agitprop and a hotbed of criminal activities. Fortunately, law enforcement agencies were largely successful in weeding out organized crime during the second half of the twentieth century, and—with the decimation of US manufacturing industries in the last forty years—blue-collar unions have <u>lost substantial political and social influence</u>[117]. However, total union membership in the US has declined by only 12 percent—from <u>16.8 million in 1975</u>[118] to <u>14.8 million in 2015</u>[119]—over that same period as a result of the <u>increasing numbers of union employees in government</u>[120].

Tragically, both blue-collar and white-collar unions continue to cling to anachronistic nineteenth-century Marxist demands for full lifetime retirement benefits after only twenty or thirty years of participation in the labor force. At a time when average human life expectancies and working careers in the US have increased by twenty to thirty years from what they were in the nineteenth century, meeting such demands is an economic impossibility and is currently responsible for bankrupting pension funds across the US in both government and industry. No competent student of US history could fail to note the ravaging and ruinous effects which the sociocommunist influence of US labor unions has had, and continues to have, on US educational and governmental institutions as well as the US economy. As highly skilled and all-too-successful extortionists, labor unions share in the blame for the exportation of US jobs to countries with lower wage scales. If globalist sociocommunists needed an excuse for their ill-conceived trade policies, labor unions surely gave them one.

Take Over Educational Institutions

It's a tragedy that sociocommunism has been permitted to insidiously spread itself throughout US educational institutions like a slow-growing cancer, where it has now metastasized into a potentially fatal malignancy. Taking their cue from Lenin, sociocommunists gradually insinuated themselves into US educational institutions until they reached the point where they can now effectively subvert most teachings contrary to their own.

For nearly one hundred years, academic tenure and globalist sociocommunist indoctrination and unionization have operated to systematically corrupt and erode US educational institutions to the point where they have become little more than factories for churning out pampered and uneducated dolts—who know nothing of US government and history, or of world government and history, yet believe they have the solutions to all the world's problems—capable of little more than spouting globalist sociocommunist agitprop. So feckless and ignorant are the graduates of these failed institutions that, without the influx of foreign students, many US STEM (science, technology, engineering, and mathematics) employers and graduate schools would be forced to close for lack of qualified applicants and candidates.

This "dumbing down" of the US population by globalist sociocommunists hell bent on overthrowing the US government is not accidental. It is, and for more than one hundred years has been, the result of a deliberate effort to weaken resistance to a sociocommunist take-over of the US by brainwashing its citizens through constant bombardment with globalist sociocommunist agitprop in the guise of education while stifling all dissenting opinion. Indeed, the devastation of US educational institutions has reached such dire proportions that they have been largely converted into globalist sociocommunist indoctrination camps—reminiscent of those established by the Cultural Revolution in Communist China—in which objective truth has been replaced by outrageous falsehoods which are protected from objective scrutiny or open debate by forced adherence to the false dogma of political correctness, and their cowering and seemingly-impotent administrators have been intimidated into acquiescing to the rankest musings and ravings of their sociocommunist faculties and their callow, pampered, and woefully-ignorant students.

At a time when faculties and students in US colleges and universities exploit their First Amendment rights to peddle their globalist sociocommunist agitprop, while abusing those same rights to shut down the rights of free speech and peaceable assembly for everyone else, the malfeasance of the administrators of US colleges and universities and the dishonorable and seditious behavior of their faculties and students are no longer amusing.

Take Over Governmental Institutions

The principal mechanisms used to achieve the sociocommunist agenda in the US have been the steady and unrelenting insinuation of Marxist-inspired ideology into labor unions and educational institutions. The spillover of subversive Marxist-inspired ideology from labor unions and educational institutions into governmental institutions and its gradual takeover of all US governmental institutions are the natural result of the increasing numbers of union employees in government, government's penchant to staff its expanding bureaucracy with recruits from leading colleges and universities, and a corresponding increase in the numbers of globalist sociocommunists and their sympathizers in both the Democrat and Republican parties—who recruit their members from the same sources.

Unfortunately, the unionization of federal government employees resulting from John Kennedy's[121] lamentable payoff to labor unions—for helping elect him to the US presidency—now provides increasing direct and indirect financial support for advancing the globalist sociocommunist agenda. It was the infamous Kennedy 1962 executive order[122] which extended unionization power to federal government employees and now provides unlimited growth potential for sociocommunist penetration into US government and saddles it with an ever-increasing impediment to accountability, effectivity, and efficiency. Interestingly, even Franklin D. Roosevelt—as evidenced by his Letter on the Resolution of Federation of Federal Employees Against Strikes in Federal Service, dated August 16, 1937[123]—recognized that government employees should never be permitted to form labor unions. Tragically, it's now fait accompli.

Take Over the Mass Media

Quickly recognized and seized upon by Woodrow Wilson and Hitler in the first two decades of the last century as the most effective and most expedient means of disseminating political agitprop, modern mass media have since evolved into a much more formidable instrument for shaping political ideologies. In an era in which radio and television news cycles are measured in hours and the Internet reduces them to minutes, modern media in conjunction with cellphones have evolved into something that could not even have been imagined one hundred years ago, namely: a universally accessible information network capable of nearly simultaneously reaching every person on the planet with potentially mesmerizing full-motion, high-fidelity, high-resolution, color-video presentations. In what could not have been envisioned in one of Wilson's or Hitler's wildest dreams, masses of unsuspecting citizens can be quickly mobilized—providing a powerful new tool for disseminating emotionally-charged political agitprop that is equally useful for alerting the public to potential dangers or for sowing political unrest and social discord.

Perhaps, due to Thomas Carlyle's[124] naive and overly optimistic view of a press corps as a kind of Fourth Estate[125]—i.e., a neutral political umpire and social safety valve that could hold an errant government in check in a society in which government officials faced periodic reelection or removal by the electorate—most US citizens trusted that the liberty of free speech in conjunction with a free press would be a sufficient safeguard to protect against protracted and unbridled political skullduggery by their government. Sadly, that trust has been misplaced, and—with the aid of modern media—broadcast news has evolved from an objective reading of the news—á la the BBC World News format—into a new kind of tabloid or yellow journalism[126] termed "infotainment," comprising one-third news and opinion; one-third unpaid advertising in the form of self-promotion by the media stars, their guests, and their networks; and one-third paid advertising—to yield an average of about ten minutes of actual news per hour of airtime. The result is an abominable and mind-numbing mixture of:

- Deliberately inflammatory, misleading, and scandalously sensationalized headlines designed to needlessly alarm and incite listeners and viewers;
- Snippets of news and factual information ranging from the banal to the obvious;
- Choreographed and scripted monotonously redundant and naive pronouncements; and
- Sound bites from "talking heads" based on incestuous interviewing of a small circle of narcissistic and obsequious associates, celebrities, coworkers, cronies, former lawyers, and judges trained as advocates, politicians, and pundits—all posing as journalists or subject experts and all taking turns promoting each other's appearances, books, celebrity, and performances to maximize their own celebrity and to fill up airtime with a steady drumbeat of insipid and naive personal biases, opinions, and masticated pabulum masquerading as journalism.

And all of it is orchestrated by media stars as physically attractive and as glamorous as any Hollywood movie star.

Sadly, infotainment editors have evolved into little more than team cheerleaders and coaches working to maximize the celebrity of their media stars—presumably for the purpose of maximizing media revenues—instead of responsibly providing an editorial check on the content of their "shows." Consequently, infotainment is a worse bargain than reruns of old Hollywood movies. At least old movie reruns provide ninety minutes of entertainment for thirty minutes of advertising, whereas infotainment provides an average of about ten minutes of news for fifty minutes of largely irrelevant prattle from talking heads. It's little wonder the average US citizen is so badly misinformed.

Alas, infotainment has become the present-day equivalent of "opium for the people," and tragically, the deliberate dumbing-down of the US citizenry by failed US educational institutions hopelessly corrupted by globalist sociocommunist activists, agitators, and their sympathizers has been so successful that the masses lap up this abomination as though it were manna from heaven. A few, like Scientific American, have warned of the dangers of blind acceptance of infotainment as fact.

> "*Knowledge is forged in the laboratory, but before it reaches the people, it passes through mediators – the government, the media and the scientific establishment – each with its own agenda. We expose an insidious practice of manipulation of news in the U.S. government and elsewhere; a culture of silence that discourages scientists from speaking out about their work; and the disconnect between what scientists do and what the public hears about. ... By using close-hold embargoes and other methods, the FDA and other institutions gain control of journalists who are supposed to keep an eye on them.*" – The Truth Brokers, a Scientific American Special Report, October 2016

However, most US citizens are woefully uncritical of media personalities impersonating subject experts. Just how woefully uncritical some have become to the pretentious ravings of charlatans and imposters was demonstrated recently, in an incident reminiscent of the Sokal affair[127], when a New Zealand professor[128] succeeded in getting gibberish—created entirely through random activations of Apple's iPhone iOS autocomplete feature—accepted as a scholarly paper for presentation at an Atlanta academic conference.

By persistently and incestuously injecting their own personas into their performances and presentations for the purposes of self-aggrandizement, self-enrichment, and self-promotion, modern media personalities lose any pretense of objectivity and quickly become political actors incapable of viewing the world in any way other than through their own personal subjective prisms. That unfortunate failing applies equally to all modern media personalities, but it especially applies to journalists.

Consequently, the only thing "elite" about the so-called "elite media" is their singular dishonesty and hypocrisy in pretending to be objective stewards of a Fourth Estate, when in fact, they are hopelessly compromised by partisan animus and exploit every opportunity to militate on behalf of their own personal agendas.[34] Only a

---

34   *"Of course, the Clintons are not only corrupt but cynical as well. They accept that the progressive media, the foundations, the universities, the bureaucracies, Hollywood, and Silicon Valley honor power more than trendy left-wing politics; they well understand that their fans will, for them, make the necessary adjustments to contextualize Clinton criminality or amorality. Sexual predations, the demonization of women, graft, and unequal protection under the law are also of no consequence to the inbred, conflicted, and morally challenged media – who will always check in with the Clinton team, like errant dogs who scratch the backdoor of their master after a periodic runaway.*

    The Clintons have contempt for the media precisely because the media are so obsequious. They smile, that, like themselves, the media are easily manipulated and compromised – to the extent of offering their articles, before publication, for Clinton approval (as the New York Times' Mark Leibovich did); leaking debate questions to the Clinton campaign (as Donna Brazile did); or saying (as Politico's chief political correspondent did), 'I have become a hack. ... Please don't share or tell anyone I did this. Tell me if I f**ked up anything.' The Clintons view such sycophants not with affection, but with disdain, given that they are moochers no better than the Clintons, with the same base desires, albeit better camouflaged by their pretense of objectivity." – The Clintons – At the End of All Things[129] by Victor Davis Hanson, *National Review*, 1 November 2016

minority of truly dedicated journalists who don't aspire to lavish life-styles are seemingly able to maintain their integrity by resisting the myriad temptations to prostitute themselves.

Media celebrity trumps all else—including competence, drive, intelligence, knowledge, skill, and talent—as a fast track to financial independence, and consequently, to a Hollywood-like ability to broadcast with complete impunity whatever drivel comes to mind regardless of how inane it might be. In the US today, where mass-media celebrity can be quickly exploited for financial and political profit, most members of the press corps, like other mass-media personalities, soon become celebrity whores. One can hardly blame members of the press corps for becoming celebrity whores—never hesitant to embarrass themselves, believing like would-be movie stars that any publicity is better than no publicity. As long as mass-media advertising continues to be the powerful catalyst that it now is for achieving personal celebrity and fortune, mass-media personalities will continue to be corrupted by it.

From constantly feeding off the celebrity, gossip, insider tips, leaks, and rumors of the ruling class, modern media personalities soon become enamored of their greater fame and fortune and aspire to the multimillion-dollar incomes of media celebrities. Knowing that personal celebrity is the largest determinant of financial success, aspiring consultants, entertainers, journalists, politicians, and pundits of all stripes soon learn to prostitute themselves to achieve greater publicity not by disrobing like Hollywood starlets but by finding a perch—like a peacock in mating season—from which to broadcast their personas. Can this descent into Hollywood-like tabloid journalism be reversed? Alas, probably not, as it's motivated solely by human greed and relies on the proven formula of the movie and music industries for maximizing celebrity and income by maximizing personal publicity.

The result has been that the US press corps has become an extension of Hollywood, i.e., an easily duped, incestuous, pretentious, pompous, sycophantic, self-congratulatory, self-important, and under-educated—albeit glamorous—assemblage comprised of celebrity wannabes who aspire to gain sufficient fame and fortune to be accepted as members of the ruling class. As such, the press corps gets vastly more credit than it deserves as an institution protective of US constitutional liberties.

In reality, the press corps is, and always has been, a double-edged sword equally exploitable for good or evil. When corrupted by money and political agendas, it can do as much public harm as good. It is free speech that is valuable and not a free press, per se. Thus, when the press corps becomes an instrument for undermining free speech, as it does when it conforms to the false dogma of political correctness, it not only becomes self-destructive by undermining its own First Amendment protections, but it becomes an unwitting or witting tool of globalist sociocommunist revolutionaries as well.

Thomas Carlyle's vain hope of a Fourth Estate is but a pipedream in a society in which the so-called "mainstream media" have evolved into a Fifth Column[35] of media stooges and political demagogues under the coercive influence of celebrity, money, and sociocommunist brainwashings. Thus, there is absolutely no chance the US press corps, as presently constituted, will ever live up to Carlyle's pipedream of a Fourth Estate as a neutral political umpire. Instead, if contemporary US experience is any indication,[36] it's rather more likely the US press corps will be the instrument which enables the ongoing globalist sociocommunist conspiracy to ultimately succeed in its efforts to overthrow the US government and install a fascist dictatorship in its place.

As noted previously, sociocommunism's track record of successfully overthrowing existing governments by insidiously brainwashing children and exploiting mass media is a twentieth-century phenomenon without historical precedent. It's no coincidence then that the greatest danger to preservation of the US as a constitutional democratic republic is now embodied in its conscripted and corrupted

---

[35] "The press should be not only a collective propagandist and a collective agitator, but also a collective organizer of the masses." – Vladimir Ilyich Ulyanov, aka Lenin

[36] "*You know the world is upside down when hackers are uncovering scandals and MSM* [mainstream media] *'journalists' are trying to cover them up.*" –JamesFuqua@Archangel3550 #CNNBlackout

mass media. Alas, the state of the US press corps, which continues to dominate US mass media, is so deplorable and disreputable that concerned citizens are forced to wonder whether it's not already too late to save the republic.

CAN THE CONTAGION
BE STOPPED?

Precisely because it has been crafted by some of the world's most evil and misguided—albeit brilliant—revolutionary minds as the most expedient means of exploiting intrinsic human weaknesses to foment social revolution, sociocommunism presents the greatest challenge to civilized government the world has ever faced. Its natural appeal to the young and naive is so great that the sociocommunism disease can't be ignored, nor will it be defeated without concerted effort. It must be confronted head on by breaking its grip on US educational and governmental institutions, by truly educating children, and by refusing to allow them to be brainwashed in the guise of education.

When US college and university campuses and big-city streets are repeatedly clogged with throngs of children—possessing only the slightest knowledge of the real world in which they live—hysterically screaming fanatical epithets designed to incite rebellion, it's well past time for decisive adult action. Moreover, the effort required will be more than that which results from new faces passing through the revolving doors of the US White House. What has taken sociocommunists nearly one hundred years to accomplish is not going to be undone in four or eight years, and certainly not without heroic effort.

Unfortunately, as noted by Bertrand Russell[130] in *WHY MEN FIGHT*[131], "*Those who have long been in the habit of exercising power become autocratic and quarrelsome, incapable of regarding an equal otherwise than as a rival.*" Others who have noted the same human weakness have put it differently with even broader applicability.

"Power tends to corrupt, and absolute power corrupts absolutely. Great [i.e., powerful] *men are almost always bad men, even when they exercise influence and not authority, still more when you superadd the tendency or the certainty of corruption by authority. There is no worse heresy than that the office sanctifies the holder of it."* John Dalberg-Acton[132]

The tendency of power to corrupt those who hold it operates in every organization and is no less evident in educational and governmental institutions. What is worse is that, by availing themselves of unassailable job security, US educational and governmental institutions have built up formidable defenses against attempts to reform them. Consequently, any attempt to reform them surely will be met with fierce resistance, and actual reform will be an arduous and long painstaking process. With concerted effort, the damage might be undone in less time than the nearly one hundred years it has taken sociocommunists to stealthily and systematically infiltrate and corrupt US educational and governmental institutions, but it surely will take decades to replace all the globalist sociocommunist ideologues in US educational and governmental institutions with competent and fair-minded individuals committed to needed reforms.

Exploit the Promise of the Internet

The Internet is, among other things, a public electronic backyard fence with persistent memory that is not easily controlled by governments or special interests and provides a vehicle for freely disseminating—digitally and at the speed of light—uncensored information to the entire world. Thus, the Internet is the only worldwide mass medium yet devised that is almost completely free and makes no claim for the accuracy or veracity of the information disseminated. As such, the Internet is a kind of public information sewer which, like other mass media, can be exploited for good or evil. Its potential applications are too many to be easily enumerated, but they include use, or abuse, as an almost-completely free and uncensored public broadcast and publishing medium for anyone seeking an audience.

Consequently, it's a perfect vehicle for transforming the failed brick-and-mortar educational model—in which teacher compensation is heavily dependent on labor-union seniority and tenure protections—to the modern media-star compensation model in which performers' compensation is determined primarily by their popularity with paying customers. As there are no labor-union seniority or tenure protections in the media-star compensation model, it would be the most expedient means, and perhaps the only practical means, of bringing real competition to public education.

Historically, entertainment and news media have not been free, and the so-called "free press" was never really free as it was always captive to financial interests. However, the modern Internet is fully capable of disseminating both entertainment and news, and—as it's almost completely free and uncensored—the Internet is a perfect vehicle for breaking up the woefully-biased and corrupted mass-media oligopolies which have become little more than instruments for disseminating globalist sociocommunist agitprop. Indeed, the sociocommunist agenda of fomenting social revolution has been greatly facilitated through the insidious brainwashings of an unwary public resulting from constant bombardment by sociocommunist agitprop broadcast through modern media.[37] Together with the globalist sociocommunist take-over of

---

[37]   *"By far the most effective branch of political education, which in this connection is best expressed by the word 'propaganda,' is carried on by the Press. The Press is the chief means employed in the process of political 'enlightenment.' It represents a kind of school for adults. This educational activity, however, is not in the hands of the State but in the clutches of powers which are partly of a very inferior character. While still a young man in Vienna I had excellent opportunities for coming to know the men who owned this machine for mass instruction, as well as those who supplied it with the ideas it distributed. At first I was quite surprised when I realized how little time was necessary for this dangerous Great Power within the State to produce a certain belief among the public; and in doing so the genuine will and convictions of the public were often completely misconstrued. It took the Press only a few days to transform some ridiculously trivial matter into an issue of national importance, while vital problems were completely ignored or filched and hidden away from public attention."* – Adolf Hitler, *MEIN KAMPF*

US educational and governmental institutions, evolution of the "mainstream media" from Fourth Estate to Fifth Column is what has enabled sociocommunists to precipitate the present constitutional crisis.

Interestingly, the Internet may be leveling the playing field in the broadcast industries. While it's still too early to know how far the trend will carry, there are hopeful signs that the old media oligopolies are under financial pressure from Internet-based competition. If the Donald Trump administration sets a precedent and forgoes the usual White House fealty to the world's largest media outlets and bypasses them via social media networks, it would be a watershed development that could herald the beginning of a new era in which broadcast media aren't easily dominated by any one political faction.

Build the Needed Political Conviction, Courage, and Leadership

With the Republican Party controlling 67 of the 98 partisan state legislative chambers[133] in the US, now could be an opportune time to move forward with amendments to the US Constitution. Will the Donald Trump administration be up to the challenge and marshal the support needed to amend the US Constitution, return the country to federalism, turn back the sociocommunist tide, and drain the Washington swamp by cutting back its bloated federal bureaucracies? Or will this be just another lost opportunity?

If Trump were able to convene a constitutional convention of the states and effect the needed reforms, he could well go down in US history—together with Washington and Lincoln—as a savior of the country and one of its greatest presidents. Based on past experience, the US may well need such a savior every one hundred years or so.

In any case, monumental courage will be required just to publicly admit the scandalous governmental malfeasance responsible for the last one-hundred-plus years of sociocommunist societal rot in the US, and Herculean efforts will be required to stop it—not to mention that required to reverse it.

As "political courage" is an oxymoron except in rare circumstances, it remains to be seen whether or not the US can muster the requisite political courage. Is this one of those rare circumstances? Only time will tell.

Amend the US Constitution

From its inception, its framers well understood that the US Constitution was an experiment, and they labored mightily to provide sufficient safeguards to preserve the US as a democratic republic that would never become a democracy, per se. As contemporaries of Tytler, they were familiar with his indictment of democracy as evidenced by Benjamin Franklin's[134] famous comment: *"A Republic, if you can keep it."*[38]

However, the framers did not foresee, and could not have foreseen, the development of labor unions or their exploitation by an insidious globalist sociocommunist conspiracy; or that judicial appointments could last for more than two decades; or that the accountability, effectivity, and efficiency of government bureaucracies would be hamstrung by ill-conceived civil-service laws and sociocommunist labor unions; nor could they have foreseen a time when the US would become so affluent that it could afford a parasitic political class totally dependent on the government for its livelihood.

Given their total lack of firsthand experience with democracy, labor unions, and sociocommunism, the framers can be forgiven if their safeguards fell short of what is required. Whether the framers of the US Constitution were over-proud of their achievement or simply failed to comprehend how dramatically US society could change over hundreds of years is unimportant.

What is important is that the time has come to make some needed changes to the US Constitution. Interestingly, that the US Constitution needs to be changed is, perhaps, the one thing conser-

---

[38] Rejoinder by Benjamin Franklin when queried *"Well, Doctor, what have we got – a Republic or a Monarchy?"* as he left Independence Hall at the close of the Constitutional Convention of 1787

vatives and globalist sociocommunists can agree on. The difference is that the changes needed to preserve the Constitution are the exact opposite of what is wanted by the globalist sociocommunists who want to destroy it.

In any case, the constitutional amendment process is outdated and needs to be updated to make it more difficult for a relatively-small minority to block needed changes. As permanent reforms will require multiple amendments to the US Constitution, a good starting point would be to pass the following twelve amendments, the first ten of which have been previously proposed by Mark Levin. [135]

1. An amendment to permit the states to propose constitutional amendments without convening a convention and to have proposed amendments ratified with the support of two-thirds of the states (instead of three-fourths)

2. An amendment limiting US Congressional service to twelve years

3. Repeal of the Seventeenth Amendment to restore the power to elect state senators to state legislators

4. An amendment limiting all judiciary appointments to one twelve-year term, and granting both Congress and state legislatures the authority to overturn court decisions with the vote of three-fifths of both houses of Congress or state legislative bodies

5. A balanced budget amendment limiting spending to 17.5 percent of the GDP and requiring a three-fifths vote to raise the debt ceiling

6. An amendment to limit and sunset federal regulations and subject the existence of all federal departments to stand-alone reauthorization bills every three years

7. An amendment clarifying that the commerce clause grants only the power to prevent states from impeding commerce among other states and that it does not grant the power to actively regulate and control commercial activities, per se

8. An amendment to limit Federal power to take private property

9. An amendment to allow states to override federal statutes by majority vote in two-thirds of state legislatures

10. An amendment to require photo identification for all federal elections and to limit early voting

11. An amendment that limits the power of US presidents to single-handedly set policies that undermine the governments of sovereign states—which in reality are acts of war

12. An amendment which requires that Congress shall make no law that applies to the citizens of the United States that does not apply equally to all members of Congress; and Congress shall make no law that applies to members of Congress that does not apply equally to all citizens of the United States.

Additionally, it will be necessary to:

- Break the globalist sociocommunist death grip on US educational institutions by:
  - *Exploiting the Internet to privatize all education, to destroy the brick-and-mortar monopoly of existing educational institutions, and to get government entirely out of the education business, and*
  - *Exploiting the star-based compensation model employed in mass-media industries to attract and retain the world's finest teachers*
- Break the death grip that labor unions currently have on governmental institutions
- To reinstate parts, if not all, of the <u>Sedition Act of 1918</u>[136] to establish criminal penalties for individuals or organizations interfering with the First-Amendment rights of others or promoting the overthrow of the US government
- To eliminate the prohibition against firing civil-service bureaucrats, and

- To require that all organizations receiving federal financial support employ merit-based employee-compensation systems devoid of seniority and tenure protections.

CONCLUSION

The citizens of every country that have previously allowed an infestation of sociocommunism to metastasize within its borders have lived to regret it, with the citizens of <u>Venezuela</u>[137] only the most-recent example. Will the US be different? If so, why? Where is the evidence, if any, to support such a contention? Surely the Joseph McCarthy experience argues against it.

Benjamin Franklin's famous quip that *"an ounce of prevention is better than a pound of cure"* may well be true, but the US lost the opportunity for prevention more than fifty years ago when it failed to combat the sociocommunist contagion that was rapidly spreading through its educational and governmental institutions. Growing up as a young man in Wisconsin in the 1930s, which was then a hotbed for incubating sociocommunist ideology,[39] McCarthy's inarticulate but intuitive understanding of the dangers inherent in sociocommunism was not widely shared in the 1950s, and his ill-conceived efforts to turn back the growing sociocommunist tide utterly failed and, in retrospect, well may have been counterproductive. In any case, it's indelibly clear that the seeds of sociocommunism that were planted in the 1930s in the big cities of the so-called "blue states" in the

---

[39] *"Progressivism became popular throughout the U.S. in the 1930s. Progressive Wisconsin professor of economics John R. Commons trained Edwin Witte, who authored the 1935 Social Security act. Wisconsin Progressives drafted much of Franklin Roosevelt's New Deal. La Follette and Wisconsin's Progressives inspired John F. Kennedy's 'New Frontier' and Lyndon Johnson's 'Great Society' programs."—* Wisconsin Historical Society, <u>*Progressivism and the Wisconsin Idea*</u>[138]

US have long since taken root as perennial sources of sociocommu-nist-inspired political agitation and social unrest.

What is worse is that the cancerous sociocommunism disease has metastasized in US educational and governmental institutions. Consequently, the US is now faced with the equivalent of terminal cancer. Can a cure for the sociocommunism rot now afflicting the US be found? If so, can it be found in time to save the Republic? Few things are certain in life, but several candidates top the list:

- Any cure is certain to require an end to the globalist socio-communist brainwashing of US children in the guise of education;
- Any cure is certain to require a long time to repair the present damage in our educational and governmental institutions;
- Any cure is certain to be expensive;
- Any cure is certain to be painful; and
- Failure to find a cure is certain to end with the demise of the democratic republic conceived by the country's founders.

It's a pity more citizens of this once-great country don't have a better appreciation for the priceless freedoms they enjoy due to the prescience of the country's founders in incorporating them into the US Constitution. Evidently, it's impossible for the coddled, ignorant, sheltered, and spoiled to appreciate either the importance or the rar-ity of the freedoms they take for granted on a daily basis. Indeed, globalist sociocommunists appear to be all too willing to squander those freedoms in attempts to legislate their utopian fantasies into existence through Orwellian social engineering.

What Is at Stake

It will be a tragedy of biblical proportions if US citizens cannot learn from the examples provided by the many twentieth-century sociocommunist atrocities and failures and rouse themselves to recognize the sociocommunist conspiracy that has been eating away at the country's foundation for more than one hundred years and put a stop to it. What a tragedy it will be for humankind if the US cannot shake off the self-induced human failing so succinctly captured in George Santayana's admonition: "*Those who cannot remember the past are condemned to repeat it*"—and learn from the examples of others who have gone before us.

In acknowledging contributors to his book *CRISIS AND LEVIATHAN*, Robert Higgs included the following assessment by a former mentor:

> "*Any society that entails the strengthening of the state apparatus by giving it unchecked control over the economy, and reunites the polity and the economy, is an historical regression. In it there is no more future for the public, or for the freedoms it supported, than there was under feudalism.*" Alvin W. Gouldner[139]

Unless the one-hundred-plus years of sociocommunist societal rot in the US can be somehow redressed, Gouldner's quote could well serve as an epitaph for the US as originally constituted by its founders. Freedom is not free, nor has it ever been free.

ENDNOTES

1. https://en.wikipedia.org/wiki/List_of_wars_by_death_toll
2. https://faculty.history.wisc.edu/sommerville/351/351-012.htm
3. https://en.wikipedia.org/wiki/David_Horowitz
4. https://en.wikipedia.org/wiki/Norman_Podhoretz
5. https://en.wikipedia.org/wiki/Vladimir_Lenin
6. https://simple.wikipedia.org/wiki/From_each_according_to_his_ability,_to_each_according_to_his_need
7. http://www.abrahamlincolnonline.org/lincoln/speeches/gettysburg.htm
8. https://en.wikipedia.org/wiki/Abraham_Lincoln
9. https://en.wikipedia.org/wiki/Charlton_Heston
10. http://alumnus.caltech.edu/~marcsulf/heston.html
11. http://www.npr.org/templates/story/story.php?storyId=141164708
12. https://en.wikipedia.org/wiki/Angelo_Codevilla
13. https://spectator.org/39326_americas-ruling-class-and-perils-revolution/
14. https://en.wikipedia.org/wiki/Peggy_Noonan
15. https://www.wsj.com/articles/trump-and-the-rise-of-the-unprotected-1456448550
16. http://www.claremont.org/crb/basicpage/after-the-republic/
17. http://www.econlib.org/library/Mises/msS0.html
18. http://images.hemmings.com/wp-content/uploads/2013/06/Packardplant_03_1500.jpg
19. https://en.wikipedia.org/wiki/Barack_Obama

20 https://www.google.com.ph/search?q=Marshall+Plan&cad=h
21 https://en.wikipedia.org/wiki/Woodrow_Wilson
22 http://cw.routledge.com/textbooks/0415311330/resources/case/02.pdf
23 https://en.wikipedia.org/wiki/Jimmy_Carter
24 http://www.apfn.org/apfn/reserve.htm
25 https://en.wikipedia.org/wiki/Milton_Friedman
26 https://en.wikipedia.org/wiki/Anna_Schwartz
27 https://en.wikipedia.org/wiki/A_Monetary_History_of_the_United_States
28 http://www.econlib.org/library/Enc/bios/Friedman.html
29 https://en.wikipedia.org/wiki/Thomas_Jefferson
30 https://www.thebalance.com/who-owns-the-u-s-national-debt-3306124
31 https://inflationdata.com/articles/2013/03/21/food-price-inflation-1913/
32 http://www.nber.org/chapters/c2287.pdf
33 https://tradingeconomics.com/united-states/wages-in-manufacturing
34 https://books.google.com/books?id=lDF_uNIWQ_oC&printsec=frontcover&dq=money+mischief&hl=en&sa=X&ved=0ahUKEwiVnODE7MnQAhVs0YMKHbNMCq4Q6AEIHTAA#v=onepage&q=money%20mischief&f=false
35 https://coinvalues.com/saint-gaudens-double-eagle/1913
36 https://en.wikipedia.org/wiki/Albert_Einstein
37 https://books.google.com.ph/books?id=vLm4oojTPnkC&pg=PA54&lpg=PA54&dq=%22The+frightful+dilemma+of+the+political+world%22+AND+Einstein&source=bl&ots=NyycEaLD_t&sig=Pc0E9zEm1cb2ggysEndI7idvpCI&hl=en&sa=X&redir_esc=y#v=onepage&q=%22The%20frightful%20dilemma%20of%20the%20political%20world%22%20AND%20Einstein&f=false
38 http://exhibits.hsl.virginia.edu/eugenics/2-origins/
39 http://www.conservapedia.com/George_Bernard_Shaw
40 https://books.google.com/books?id=XdTkDAAAQBAJ&pg=PT47&dq=%22As+to+socialism,+unless+it+is+internation-

al%22&hl=en&sa=X&ved=0ahUKEwjl-tuvq8rQAhUH5YM-KHZybA7UQ6AEIHTAA#v=onepage&q=%22As%20 to%20socialism%2C%20unless%20it%20is%20international %22&f=false

41 http://www.greatwar.nl/books/meinkampf/meinkampf.pdf

42 https://en.wikipedia.org/wiki/The_Road_to_Serfdom

43 https://en.wikipedia.org/wiki/Friedrich_Hayek

44 http://www.pbs.org/wnet/jimcrow/stories_org_democratic. html

45 https://www.depts.ttu.edu/freemarketinstitute/research/ research_crisis_papers/CrisisWithoutLeviathan.pdf

46 https://en.wikipedia.org/wiki/Robert_Higgs

47 https://en.wikipedia.org/wiki/Adolf_Hitler

48 http://www.claremont.org/crb/basicpage/after-the-republic/

49 http://www.nationalreview.com/article/420321/democratic-party-racist-history-mona-charen

50 https://en.wikipedia.org/wiki/Edward_M._House

51 https://en.wikipedia.org/wiki/Franklin_D._Roosevelt

52 http://galton.org/

53 http://progressingamerica.blogspot.com/2012/03/wood-row-wilson-and-eugenics-he.html

54 https://en.wikipedia.org/wiki/J._Robert_Oppenheimer

55 https://www.voltairenet.org/IMG/pdf/House_Philip_Dru__Administrator.pdf

56 http://spectator.org/articles/39326/americas-ruling-class-and-perils-revolution

57 http://www.visionandvalues.org/docs/Kengor_Great_Depression _and_American_Communist_Party.pdf

58 https://en.wikipedia.org/wiki/Joseph_McCarthy

59 http://www.econlib.org/library/Mises/msS0.html

60 https://en.wikipedia.org/wiki/Ludwig_von_Mises

61 https://en.wikipedia.org/wiki/Dinesh_D'Souza

62 https://theindependentwhig.com/2016/09/01/the-urban-plantation/

63 https://en.wikipedia.org/wiki/Lyndon_B._Johnson

64 http://www.washingtontimes.com/news/2014/may/21/ editorial-the-not-so-great-society/
65 https://en.wikipedia.org/wiki/George_Washington
66 https://www.ourdocuments.gov/doc.php?flash=false& doc=15&page=transcript
67 http://www.heretical.com/miscella/dinform.html
68 https://en.wikipedia.org/wiki/Niccol%C3%B2_Machiavelli
69 https://en.wikipedia.org/wiki/Saul_Alinsky
70 http://www.dailymail.co.uk/news/article-3970082/How-Captain-Robert-Scott-s-log-book-expedition-Antarctica-100-years-ago-raises-troubling-new-doubts-global-warming.html
71 https://en.wikipedia.org/wiki/Committee_on_Public_Information
72 http://www.propagandacritic.com/articles/ww1.cpi.html
73 https://en.wikipedia.org/wiki/Reich_Ministry_of_Public_Enlightenment_and_Propaganda
74 https://en.wikipedia.org/wiki/H._L._Mencken
75 http://www.econlib.org/library/Mises/msS0.html
76 https://www.youtube.com/watch?v=Cf2nqmQIfxc
77 https://www.christianforums.com/threads/wsj-bomb-tex-as-the-psychological-roots-of-anti-americanism.32336/
78 http://www.freerepublic.com/focus/f-news/885796/posts
79 https://www.wsj.com/articles/millennials-vs-mutant-capitalism-1476831817
80 https://www.wsj.com/articles/is-communism-cool-ask-a-millennial-1482450940
81 http://www.historynet.com/was-the-usa-ever-no-1-in-education.htm
82 https://rankingamerica.wordpress.com/category/rankings/ranking-of-11-to-20-rankings/
83 https://en.wikipedia.org/wiki/Theodore_Dalrymple
84 http://archive.frontpagemag.com/readArticle.aspx?ARTID=7445
85 https://en.wikipedia.org/wiki/Ronald_Reagan
86 https://en.wikipedia.org/wiki/Evil_empire

87 http://www.usatoday.com/story/news/politics/elections/2016/2016/10/31/thiel-what-trump-represents-isnt-crazy-and-s-not-going-away/93066868/

88 https://en.wikipedia.org/wiki/350.org

89 https://en.wikipedia.org/wiki/Al_Gore

90 https://en.wikipedia.org/wiki/Bill_McKibben

91 https://en.wikipedia.org/wiki/Greenpeace

92 https://en.wikipedia.org/wiki/James_Hansen

93 https://en.wikipedia.org/wiki/Sierra_Club

94 https://en.wikipedia.org/wiki/Dwight_D._Eisenhower

95 http://www.americanrhetoric.com/speeches/dwightdeisenhowerfarewell.html

96 https://encyclopedia.1914-1918-online.net/article/war_industries_board

97 https://en.wikipedia.org/wiki/Alexander_Fraser_Tytler,_Lord_Woodhouselee

98 https://en.wikipedia.org/wiki/Winston_Churchill

99 https://books.google.com/books?id=2h1LAQAAMAAJ&pg=PA219&lpg=PA219&dq=%22nothing+better+than+an+Utopian+theory,+a+splendid+chimera,+descriptive+of+a+state+of+society+that+never+did,+and+never+could+exist%22&source=bl&ots=_57tUunq3X&sig=Vmohx-qe2rnT-dt7nclFczLzcL3A&hl=en&sa=X&ved=0ahUKEwip6aPcorvQAhVO1GMKHZs0AVMQ6AEIGzAA#v=onepage&q=%22nothing%20better%20than%20an%20Utopian%20theory%2C%20a%20splendid%20chimera%2C%20descriptive%20of%20a%20state%20of%20society%20that%20never%20did%2C%20and%20never%20could%20exist%22&f=false

100 https://en.wikipedia.org/wiki/Chris_Argyris

101 http://www.accel-team.com/human_relations/hrels_06ii_argyris.html

102 https://en.wikipedia.org/wiki/Benjamin_Spock

103 https://en.wikipedia.org/wiki/Young_Communist_International

104 http://www.historyplace.com/worldwar2/hitleryouth/hj-beginnings.htm

105 http://www.nclr.org/

DAVID L. R. STEIN

106 https://en.wikipedia.org/wiki/John_Maynard_Keynes
107 http://cas.umkc.edu/economics/people/facultypages/kregel/courses/econ645/winter2011/generaltheory.pdf
108 http://nypost.com/2016/12/14/nasa-scientist-warns-earth-is-due-for-extinction-level-event/
109 https://www.washingtonpost.com/news/speaking-of-science/wp/2017/06/21/stephen-hawking-calls-for-a-return-to-the-moon-as-earths-clock-runs-out/
110 http://www.space.com/34184-stephen-hawking-afraid-alien-civilizations.html
111 https://en.wikipedia.org/wiki/William_F._Buckley_Jr.
112 https://en.wikipedia.org/wiki/Robert_Michels
113 http://www.ideasinactiontv.com/tcs_daily/2005/09/the-iron-law-of-oligarchy-revisited.html
114 https://en.wiktionary.org/wiki/politia
115 https://en.wikipedia.org/wiki/Russification
116 https://en.wikipedia.org/wiki/Languages_of_the_Soviet_Union
117 http://www2.ucsc.edu/whorulesamerica/power/history_of_labor_unions.html
118 http://digitalcommons.ilr.cornell.edu/cgi/viewcontent.cgi?article=1176&context=key_workplace
119 http://www.bls.gov/news.release/pdf/union2.pdf
120 http://www.cnsnews.com/news/article/terence-p-jeffrey/21955000-12329000-government-employees-outnumber-manufacturing
121 https://en.wikipedia.org/wiki/John_F._Kennedy
122 https://www.flra.gov/50th_Anniversary_EO10988
123 http://www.presidency.ucsb.edu/ws/?pid=15445
124 https://en.wikipedia.org/wiki/Thomas_Carlyle
125 https://en.wikipedia.org/wiki/Fourth_Estate
126 https://manshipmassmedia.wordpress.com/2014/11/14/modern-day-yellow-journalism/
127 https://en.wikipedia.org/wiki/Sokal_affair

128 http://www.nydailynews.com/news/national/paper-written-autocomplete-accepted-academic-conference-article-1.2841860

129 http://www.nationalreview.com/article/441637/hillary-bill-clinton-greed-corruption-power-cynicism-endlessly

130 https://en.wikipedia.org/wiki/Bertrand_Russell

131 C:\Users\dstein\Desktop\Why Men Fight.pdf

132 https://en.wikipedia.org/wiki/John_Dalberg-Acton,_1st_Baron_Acton

133 http://www.cnsnews.com/news/article/barbara-hollingsworth/after-winning-7-more-seats-gop-dominance-state-legislatures-all

134 https://en.wikipedia.org/wiki/Benjamin_Franklin

135 https://en.wikipedia.org/wiki/Mark_Levin

136 http://legal-dictionary.thefreedictionary.com/Alien+and+Sedition+Acts

137 https://www.wsj.com/articles/venezuela-is-starving-1493995317:

138 https://www.wisconsinhistory.org/Records/Article/CS417

139 http://www.rebelyid.com/tag/alvin-gouldner/

About the Author

David L. R. (Dave) Stein,
Serial Entrepreneur (retired)

Dave Stein lives in Austin, Texas. He is a computer-industry and start-up veteran. Over the last fifty years Dave has been a director of ten high-technology start-up companies, including four with combined revenues of more than $1 billion that he cofounded. His track record includes twenty years in the computer industry in a variety of engineering, sales, marketing, and general management positions at Control Data, IBM, Scientific Data Systems, Univac, Systems Engineering Laboratories, and Harris Corporation. In 1979, he cofounded Gartner Inc. where he managed all operations from day one, grew recurring revenues to $40 million in six years, and established Gartner's franchise as the global leader in strategic IT consulting services. In 1985, he cofounded a $250 million venture-capital partnership in Southern California. From 1992 to 2004, he was a management consultant in San Jose. From 2004 to 2016, he was cofounder of two start-up software companies. He received a BS degree with distinction in Mathematics and Physics and did graduate work in Mathematics at the University of Minnesota Institute of Technology.